AUTOMOBILE RESTORATION GUIDE
—3rd Edition

by Stanley Nowak

MODERN AUTOMOTIVE SERIES

TAB BOOKS Inc.

BLUE RIDGE SUMMIT. PA. 17214

THIRD EDITION

FIRST PRINTING

Copyright © 1981 by TAB BOOKS Inc.

Printed in the United States of America

Library of Congress Cataloging in Publication Data

Nowak, Stanley, 1926-
Automobile restoration guide, for all antique, classic, special interest.

(Modern sports car series)
1. Automobiles—Restoration. I. Title.
TL 151.1.N68   1977   629.28'8'22   77-25533
ISBN 0-8306-9994-5
ISBN 0-8306-2101-6 (pbk.)

Cover photo courtesy of Ford Motor Company.

Table Of Contents

Introduction

If you're past the point of deciding to buy an old car and past the point of searching for and acquiring the old car of your dreams, you're ready to explore the multitudinous mysteries of restoration. For you, it's too late to reconsider. You're committed. And this book will help you decide if you should do the work yourself, have it done professionally, or strike a middle course, some "do it yourself" and some professional work.

If you haven't yet bought that old car, you will find this book even more valuable, as it will help you decide if restoring an old car is something you should get involved in. Can you afford it? Do you have the spare time to devote to it? Do you have a place to work? Will your family be sympathetic and cooperative? How much will it cost? How much time will it require? How much research is required? How perfect does a restoration have to be? What tools will you need and how much will they cost? Where do you go to get parts required or replaced? And most important, *what* car should you restore?

In philosophical terms, this book will not dictate any "best way" of restoring an old car. It will simply give you the options and let you decide the "best way" in terms of your own personal needs, desires and limitations.

Good luck!

Stanley Nowak

Acknowledgments

Special thanks for helping produce this book are due to: My wife, Adele, for her special patience and understanding.

Road & Track for publishing the article which inspired this volume.

Don Lefferts, Manager, Vintage Auto Restorations Inc., Ridgefield, Connecticut, who supplied many of the photographs and contributed his knowledge and experience.

Robert Turnquist, Manager, Hibernia Auto Restorations Inc., Hibernia, New Jersey, who supplied photographs.

Ernest and Bob Swanson, Ridgefield, Connecticut, for their help and cooperation on Model A matters.

Chuck Nesbitt, Restoration Manager of Grand Prix SSR Co., E. Setauket, Long Island, New York, who helped in revising this book.

Chapter 1
What To Buy:
Emotion Versus Investment

Don't be afraid to buy your first old car for emotional, sentimental reasons. The most famous automobile collector in the world, the late Bill Harrah, bought his first car, a Maxwell, because of the happy memories he associated with it. Today, his collection of automobiles, the largest in the world, is located in Reno, Nevada, and is well worth a detour to see.

Try a Ford

If you do have a sentimental favorite, chances are it's a Ford. Perhaps it is a Model A like the one I bought in high school for $50 and sold a year later for $75. Or could it be the '57 Ford Thunderbird you longingly admired but could never afford. Don't worry, your instincts were right. Stick to an old Ford and you'll never be hurt. Well, at least your chances of being hurt are greatly diminished (See Fig. 1-1).

The "old Ford" section of the hobby is enormous. Of the estimated 350,000 car owners in the hobby, probably one-third of them are involved with Fords of one kind or another. This massive interest has created a commercially important demand for Ford parts, Ford services, Ford literature, and Ford restoration specialists. Dozens of profit-minded enthusiasts have sought and discovered "New Old Stock" (NOS, as it is referred to in the classified ads). These are original, new parts made by Ford. In addition, most parts that are in demand are being reproduced.

Many are so well made that they are difficult to separate from the genuine NOS.

Even more important to you is the large and growing market involved in the buying and selling of old Fords. Literally hundreds are offered for sale every month. This amount of constant competitive activity establishes firm prices, lessens the risk of "getting stuck" and, if you should change your mind, ensures a sale at a fair price within a reasonably short time. The final argument in favor of Fords is price. An unrestored one in poor condition can be bought for as little as a few hundred dollars and the finest restored Fords go for well under $25,000, about as inexpensive as you will find in the old car hobby.

If the Fords are safe investments then the riskiest cars to buy must be all those that are little known and of no technical importance. The 1905 Pungs Finch (owned by Austin Clark's Long Island Automotive Museum, Southampton, New York) is certainly a little known car make, but it is very valuable because of its superb workmanship, heroic size (610 cubic inches), and advanced engineering features (overhead valves and overhead camshaft).

Rare not Necessarily Good

The real losers are the dozens of uninteresting, inexpensive, assembled cars that were ground out in the United States between 1915 and 1930. At the risk of offending some owners, I must list a few of the cars which are noteworthy for their total lack of redeeming features: Corinthian, Drummond, Fremont, Hackett, Huffman, Marshall, and Olympian are some of the makes in this category. Their lack of desirability is not enhanced by their rarity. This is the type of car which is least interesting to the collector. Parts are almost impossible to obtain and resale may take years.

Between the Fords and the Fremonts is a vast middle ground of well-made, well-engineered automobiles, some with ingenious technical features, which are well worth restoring provided you have the patience and determination to see them through to completion. Don't pass up a car because you never heard of it. First, look it up in *The Complete Encyclopedia of Motor Cars*, edited by G.N. Georgano, available in most public libraries. This will give you a thumbnail sketch of the car's history and unusual features, a basis on which to judge its potential. More detailed information will have to be obtained from owners of the particular make, editors of club magazines, club specialists, and libraries specializing in automobiles, such as the Detroit Public Library, automotive history collection, 5201 Woodward Ave., Detroit, MI 48202.

Fig. 1-1. A safe investment! A lovely 1931 Model A Ford Roadster restored for "show or go" by owner. Owner: Ernest Swanson, Ridgefield, CT.

The "Great Classics"

If you are able to invest in one of the "great classics," you may find it rewarding to talk to a professional in the field of buying and selling the best old cars, such as Ed Jurist, who owns the Vintage Car Store in Nyack, NY, and who has steered his steady customers into the great cars for over 20 years. Mr. Jurist keeps a file on every car he has sold and these records document the monumental extent of his foresight. He strongly recommends the purchase of cars which were acknowledged "the best" when they were new; cars fitted with the bodywork of the most outstanding coachbuilders of their day, cars that were acknowledged as outstanding for their workmanship and engineering at the time they were built.

A definitive list of these "great cars" is not possible, for as the list grows the selection becomes more subjective and the choice more financially speculative. Rolls Royce, Bentley, Duesenberg, Packard, Mercedes, Cadillac, Bugatti, Stutz, Mercer, Simplex, Ferrari are undisputed great cars but even a Rolls Royce can be a poor investment if it is the low powered 20HP model bearing 4-door sedan coachwork that is aesthetically displeasing. The sex appeal of the coachwork is an overriding factor in determining present value and future appreciation potential. The most desirable are the 4-door touring cars and the dual-cowl phaetons (with a windshield for the rear passengers as well as the front) are the ultimate in this category. From this pinnacle, the order of value descends: roadster, convertible, coupe, town car, sedan, limousine, hearse.

Until recently the "great cars" made before World War II were the best investments. During the period 1967 through 1977 Duesenbergs appreciated over 1000 percent! So did Bugattis. These are among the "classic cars" as defined by the Classic Car Club of America. This well organized national club specializes in cars made between 1925 and World War II, and the list of cars they have decided are "classic" is found in Appendix B.

Until about two years ago, the cars which were the most expensive ones appreciated at the highest rates. This is no longer true. And at the present time these cars have leveled off in value and are appreciating only at the rate of inflation. Prior to 1978 every car which sold at a record price had appreciated five to 10 times as much as the average old car sold at the same time! A Duesenberg Coupe de Ville which sold for $5000 in 1960 was purchased in 1978 for about $200,000. A Type 59 Grand Prix Bugatti which sold for $7500 in 1962 appreciated to about

$300,000. A Bugatti Type 57SC Atlantic which sold at auction seven years ago for $69,000 was worth over $300,000 two years ago. These cars have appreciated in the last two years. But only at the rate of about 10% each year.

Milestone Cars

Since 1978, collectors looking for maximum appreciation have gravitated to post-war automobiles. The Milestone Car Society specializes in this period with a cutoff after 1967. A list of their certified "milestone" cars is included in Appendix B. In a sense, The Milestone Society is trying to guess which of the more recently produced cars will become true classics in the future. To help them with the guessing game, they have entrusted the selection of "milestone" cars to a board of distinguished experts whose choices are finally approved or disapproved by a vote of the membership. If you agree with them and want to back it up with cash you can start buying 1949 and 1963 through 1965 Buick Rivieras, any Rolls Royce, 1961 through 1967 Lincoln Continentals, 1953 through 1956 Packard Caribbeans, 1967 Cadillac Eldorados, and so on. The full list is a great conversation piece as it never fails to arouse disagreement. From an investment point of view it presents most interesting possibilities. The stakes are not too high and if you guess right, the rewards can be great. Meanwhile, you have a car which can be used for every day transportation, and you can preserve it at the same time.

Sports/Racing Cars

If post-war cars appeal to you, The Milestone Car Society is not the only game in town. For example, the Vintage Sports Car Club of America encourages the preservation of post-war sports/racing cars by issuing a list of those "eligible" to compete in their hillclimbs, races, and concours. Most rare and unusual sports cars and racing cars made before January 1, 1960, are on the "eligible" list (available on request from the secretary of the club).

The activities of this club, together with the clubs in England who sponsor post-war "historic" racing, has seen a steady appreciation in values. Ferrari sports/racing models, which were once available for $3,500 or less, are today fetching $55,000 and more. Even small displacement sports/racing cars such as the Lotus XI and Lola 1100 are selling for $15,000 to $20,000 whereas four to six years ago they could be had for under $2,000.

One-make clubs devoted to post-war cars are in abundance. Ferraris were not manufactured until after World War II and there are three good clubs devoted to their cause. For the well-heeled post-war enthusiast, the Ferrari is probably the ultimate choice. In particular, the rarer sports/racing models seem destined for maximum appreciation. If Ferraris appeal to you, join all their clubs, plunge in and learn all you can before you buy. Yes, there are Ferraris you can buy in good working order for $10,000 or less, but they are not necessarily the models that will appreciate the most. Of all the post-war cars, Ferraris are indeed a very special breed. Already some of their most desirable models have exceeded $200,000 in value. Ferrari began production in 1947 and new models are still being produced. Over the span of years, hundreds of different models and variations were produced. Indeed, it is a very complicated subject and if you are seriously interested in Ferraris you will be well advised to purchase the two most comprehensive books on the subject: *Ferrari*, by Fitzgerald and Merritt, and *Ferrari—The Man, The Machines*, published by *Automobile Quarterly Magazine*. There are, of course, a wide variety of American and foreign-made automobiles which are available at much lower prices.

Ideally, you should be able to combine an emotional choice, the car you have secretly longed for, with a car you believe will be worth more to others in the future. For most of us, the final choice will be a compromise. It must be a car whose purchase you can defend with enthusiasm. If "maximum potential appreciation" is not important to you, don't worry about it. The only lost cause in the world of automobiles is when the owner loses his enthusiasm. The late Bill Harrah's first Maxwell is still part of his world famous collection and, of course, it is worth much more than when he bought it.

Chapter 2
Car Restoration:
Your Time And Money

Most professional car restoration shops charge $25 or more per hour for their labor plus the cost of materials or services purchased outside, to which they usually add 20% for handling. If unusually hard-to-find parts are missing, you will have to pay the professional restorer for the time he devotes to finding the parts, at $25 per hour, plus the cost of the parts themselves. Or you will have to pay the cost of having them made. If the part is machined, the machinist will charge at least $30 per hour plus the cost of the raw materials. If you can do some or all of this work yourself you will save money. You can replace money spent with a professional restoration service with your own time.

When Resources Are Limited

If your own time and money are limited, you save a great deal of both by buying an old car which is 100 percent complete and original. This means doing some homework before you go out to buy. Yes, this may even mean passing up a "bargain" until you know what you are buying. In the case of a very rare and unusual car this homework is vital. Not long ago, a friend who works for a professional restoration shop, drove from New York to Boston to buy what was represented to be a 1913 Peugeot "Bebe"Roadster. What he found was a very early Austin 7 worth far less! Fortunately, he had worked on a genuine Peugeot "Bebe" and knew the car intimately. This kind of deception is rare but it does happen. If you have a limited bankroll it can be disastrous.

Do Your Own Research

The quickest way to become an "expert" on a particular make of car is to buy all the books available on the subject and join the clubs that cater to your car. Books can be ordered from the specialist book dealers listed in Appendix C and the clubs listed in Appendix B. To get the most help, join two clubs: a club devoted exclusively to your make of car, and a more general club that accepts all cars of a particular era.

Examples. If you plan to buy a 1938 Packard 180, join the Packard Owners Club and the Classic Car Club of America (the 180 model Packard is a "classic" as defined by the CCCA); if you desire a 1925 Ford Model T, join the Model T Ford Club International and the Antique Automobile Club of America or the Horseless Carriage Club, depending on which has the most active chapter in your area; if the 1951-54 Hudson Hornet is your choice, join the Hudson-Essex-Terraplane Club and The Milestone Car Society, which specializes in post-war cars and defines the 1951-54 Hudson Hornet as a "milestone car"; if you're planning to restore a 1946-49 M.G.T.C. you will want to join the M.G. "T" Register, the Vintage Sports Car Club of America, and The Milestone Car Society. A full list of the cars accepted by the Classic Car Club of America and The Milestone Car Society is included in Appendix B.

Study the books you have acquired and attend the meetings of the clubs you have joined. When, at a meeting, you see a car of the type you want to buy, introduce yourself to the owner as a new member and ask him to show you his car. Most owners are delighted to show off their cars and their expertise. If you feel you are getting along well with the owner, ask him for his name, address, and telephone number. When you are ready to buy your old car you may find that your new friend is willing to go with you to inspect the car. You will certainly find his experience invaluable in selecting a similar car and during the time the car is being restored.

Ideally, you want a car that is 100 percent complete and running. But does it really have to be 100 percent original? Who cares if the carburetor is a modern replacement? It probably works better anyway.

Collecting is Preserving

Here I must define the purpose of collecting old cars. In simplest terms, it is to preserve them. An old car is not preserved by substituting a modern carburetor for the original. Improving an old car is not necessarily preserving it. The car clubs are devoted to preserving old cars and there is no place for a 1936 Cord with a Cadillac engine in it or a 1928 Model A Ford with hydraulic brakes. Old cars that have been extensively modified should be avoided. For the most part, such cars provide only "show off" transportation and contribute nothing to the hobby or to the preservation of automobile history. We are not referring to the classic hot rod or street rod. These are legitimate facets of the automotive hobby and have no relationship to the subject of this book, the restoration and preservation of old cars.

From the standpoint of saving time and money, the perfect car to buy would be one which has been properly stored in a heated garage while it was still in "as new" original condition. Such a car would require no restoration, only further preservation! Find a car as close to this "ideal" as possible. Think ahead and you will buy with care and patience, looking for the very best in originality and condition.

Chapter 3
How To Buy An Old Car

Anyone with experience in the hobby (or business) of buying old cars will tell you the need is for plenty of hard cash, persistence, and luck. Let's consider the situation honestly. There's nothing like a roll of bills counted out on a table to separate a man from his long loved, but neglected automotive treasure. And this is exactly the kind of factor needed when you're trying to buy an old car that is *not* for sale.

Be Convincing

This is the toughest "buy" in the world. Sometimes, money alone will do it, if you have enough, but more than likely it will take something more. If you can talk to the owner you will probably be wise to pull out all the emotional stops. If you've heard of the car from a friend or neighbor you'll want a personal introduction. Find out what the owner likes, what his interests are and make use of the information. Anything you can do to assure the owner that the car will be a tribute to him is bound to help. Let him know that the car will be restored to "as new" running condition and that it will be displayed at public events with a sign giving the full history of the car and his part in its preservation.

Arrive at the owner's home in a restored old car and you will do wonders to convince him of the credibility of your story. How can anyone not be swayed by the sight of a beautiful old car which looks and runs as perfectly as the day it left the factory?

Read the Ads

Fortunately, there are plenty of old car owners who are delighted to sell their cars and these people are much easier to cope with. These cars are advertised in small local newspapers, local "buy-lines" and "mart" papers, local auto club bulletins, and in the national publications such as *Hemming's Motor News, Cars and Parts, Old Cars, Road and Truck, The New York Times, Motor Sport* (published in England), and the national auto club bulletins and magazines.

Hemming's Motor News is probably the best all around source for old cars and parts of all types. This magazine has a circulation of over 187,000 and consists of over 410 pages of classified ads with almost no editorial matter. Over half the cars offered are Fords or post-war milestone or special-interest cars (made after World War II that are not recognized by any of the major old car clubs). The rest covers the entire spectrum of automobiles made in the world. Even if you don't find the car you want, you will find Hemming's a fascinating treasure trove of automobilia of every description. For sheer quantity of old cars for sale there is nothing like it.

Cars and Parts also offers pages of classified ads similar in coverage to Hemming's but with many pages of valuable editorial material, car made histories, reprints of car catalogs, etc., and is printed on a good grade of glossy paper.

Old Cars is *the* newspaper of the old car hobby. In it you will find the best coverage of what the clubs are doing, what is happening at the old car auctions, with lists of exactly what cars are sold and for how much. It also reviews new books and includes a large section of classified ads of cars, parts, and services. If you want to subscribe to only one general publication, it is probably the best one.

Road and Track is a well-known national car enthusiast's magazine. Of all the national magazines available on newsstands everywhere it has by far the largest classified section of cars for sale. Those offered are almost entirely sports cars or luxury cars made in Europe and for this type of car it is probably the best source.

The New York Times, Sunday edition, sports section contains the automobile classified ads. Between the late model American cars and late model foreign cars is a section headed "Antique & Classic Cars," which is the largest section of its kind in any newspaper in America. Cars of every conceivable type are offered and most serious collectors in the Northeast spend every Sunday morning reading it before anything else. It is also available a day or two later in every large city in the country.

Motor Sport magazine, published in England, is a must for every foreign car lover. In addition to excellent editorial coverage of old car activities in Great Britain, it also offers a very large classified section of Rolls Royces, Bentleys, and every other make of European car. Single copies are available from R. Gordon & Co. (see under "Books and Manuals" in Appendix C).

Club magazines and bulletins are highly recommended as many club members will offer their cars first in a club publication. Particularly valuable are the magazines and bulletins offered by the Antique Automobile Club of America, the Classic Car Club of America, the Horseless Carriage Club, and the Veteran Motor Car Club of America.

Get Details

When you find a car advertised that appeals to you, telephone and ask for details of the condition of the car. Be certain to get the correct year of the car, model, type and number, and its chassis and engine numbers. This information can be invaluable when discussing the car with owners of similar automobiles or other experts on that make.

If the car is at a distant location ask for photographs. If no telephone number is given in the advertisement you will have to write the owner, but it is always better to telephone because you might want to ask the owner to hold the car for you based on the information you receive from him. A deposit of $50 to $100 will usually hold a car until you can obtain the photographs and full information on which you can base your decision to proceed with it or not.

Photographs can be very misleading. They always make a poor car look good and a perfect car look average. Either way you don't get a true picture of the car's condition from them. Moral: Don't buy any car without inspecting it personally and thoroughly.

Make a Personal Inspection

When you go to buy the car, be prepared to pay for it in full with a certified check, cash, or traveler's checks. Do not pay for a car unless you can take delivery immediately. Come prepared with a car trailer, tow bar, or, if driveable, license plates. If the owner says the car is in running condition, make it clear to him that you will want to hear the engine and have a demonstration ride before buying it. Bring a mechanic familiar with the car or the owner of a similar one and let the owner know that you will make a total and careful inspection.

Before you begin a mechanical check, find out exactly what, if anything, is not original on the car. This means a thorough survey of the car from top to bottom inside and out. Don't hesitate to bring your research material with you. Take your time, paying close and particular attention to lights, engine and transmission, rear axle, instruments, wheels (checking for correct original size), and bumpers.

Most important (and this is often overlooked) is the maker's plate on the firewall. This plate is usually stamped with the engine and chassis numbers (often two different numbers). Bring a flashlight and be sure the number stamped on the engine is the same as the "Engine Number" on the plate. If it is not the same it is very possible the engine may be unacceptable for use in club events. This means you will have to identify the engine before you can decide if the car can be considered original. In cases like this, you should get a ruling from the club to find out what is acceptable and what is not.

Mechanical Checkpoints

Once you are satisfied that the car is original you can proceed to a study of its condition. If the car is represented as being in good mechanical condition you should check the following:

●If the radiator is cold and the car starts quickly you can be sure the engine is in reasonably good condition.

●A drive of 20 minutes or more is advisable in order to be certain the cooling system is in good order and that the oil pressure is satisfactory (oil pressure information should be obtained from the owner of a similar car). This will give you the opportunity to observe the functioning of the gear shift (always ask to have the car driven in reverse for a few feet), the clutch, brakes, horn, instruments, and emergency brake (on a hill, please). Oil pressure should be steady (erratic or low oil pressure could indicate bearings about to expire).

●Noise in the engine, gearbox or rear axle should be evaluated by your "expert" companion. Some cars are noted for habitually noisy rear axles or valves.

● Compression testing of each cylinder takes only a few minutes and will reveal many serious faults in the engine. If all cylinder readings are within 10% of each other, it is likely the engine is in good condition. If one or more cylinders show no pressure or very low pressure compared to the others, you are in for trouble. At the very least, the valves will have to be inspected and probably the rings, which means a major overhaul.

●Unless the engine has been recently overhauled or has been lovingly preserved, you must count on having it rebuilt. This should be calculated as part of the cost of restoration.

●The "front end" is also important. Check for "play" in the steering. If you can move the steering wheel more than 1" at the rim before the front wheels move, you will find that it is caused by a worn steering box, worn tie rod ends, or all of them. Jack up the front of the car and check the amount of wear in the kingpins.

●Check if all the instruments and lights are in good working order. Don't forget to check the heater if there is one.

Body Condition

The condition of the body is just as important as the mechanics of the car. For a steel bodied car, the enemy is rust. Don't worry about the rust you can see; search for the rust that has not yet broken through to the surface and for the rust that has been patched with fiberglass or putty. Bring a magnet with you and try it in places you suspect will be rusted. This usually is where one panel joins another providing a low spot to catch water. Running boards and the panels below the doors are particularly susceptible to rust. Cars that have been patched with fiberglas or putty, revealed by a magnet, should be avoided.

Don't be fooled by cars made partly or wholly of aluminum because the magnet will not react to aluminum. Many of the more expensive foreign cars have moving panels (doors, hood, trunk) made of aluminum with the rest of steel. All-aluminum bodies are usually found on one-of-a-kind prototype cars and those intended for racing. These are generally considered more valuable.

What to Offer

Now comes the trickiest part of the whole transaction. What should you pay for it? And a slightly different question—what is it worth? In absolute terms, the "market" value of any given car is the price paid recently for an identical car. If you follow the old car auctions you will have the best idea of what current market values represent. The prices advertised in magazines and newspapers are "asking" prices and these must usually be discounted 10%-20% to find their real market value.

You might try the Old Cars Value Guide (listed under Magazines in Appendix C; this is published by *Old Cars* magazine). These list old cars sold at auction, privately, and by dealers specializing in old cars and they do their best to accurately describe the condition of the cars. But be warned, frequently the car model information is inaccurate: wrong year, wrong model, or wrong body style.

Buying a Restored Car

Have you thought of buying a fully restored car? If you have little time and aptitude for restoration work, a strong desire for an old car you can be proud of, and a high four-figure bank balance, you should give serious consideration to a car that has been fully restored.

Consider the economics of buying a restored car. An unrestored car will take from one to two years to complete and the cost of restoration will increase 10 percent to 15 percent each year with the final cost really impossible to calculate. A fully restored car can often be bought for last year's restoration costs. One man's folly can be another man's bargain and you will know exactly what it will cost. Appreciation on a restored car will run at the rate of 10 percent to 20 percent a year. Add to this the advantages of instant enjoyment and you have a very appealing possibility.

Whatever you decide, get as much help and advice as you can while knowing full well that the final decision will be yours to make. This is when "what is it worth?" comes to grips with "What should I pay for it?" Do your homework well. Get as much expert help as you can from the most knowledgeable enthusiasts you know. The more you know about the subject the less likely you will have reason to regret your decision.

Chapter 4
Restoration Groundwork

If you have just purchased your favorite old car in unrestored condition and have neither the time, skill nor inclination to "do it yourself" you have nothing to fear. Join the hundreds of collectors who each year entrust their out-of-date machinery to a professional restoration service.

Dealing With Professionals

The proper restoration of any automobile is an expensive proposition. Careful consideration should be made of the risks and advantages. Advice should be sought from experienced and objective sources. The depth of your investment should relate to the potential value of the car. Is your car really worth restoring? Are you prepared to accept a truthful, objective answer. What will professional restoration cost? What will your car be worth after it is restored?

If you ask well-known collectors with long experience in the economics of restoration, you will probably find they are loath to share their experience with you. Their reluctance is understandable. They don't want to divulge their mistakes such as too much money spent restoring the wrong car or trouble with the Internal Revenue Service wondering if it really is a hobby. And don't forget the wife they've been deceiving for all these years who now believes her husband is going to leave her a gold mine in old cars when most of his collection consists of worthless mid-1920s Moon, Whippet, and Maxwell cars he remembered from his youth.

On the other hand, he might be reluctant to admit that all his Duesenbergs were bought for $1200, restored for $5000 in the days when a dollar was worth at least 95¢, and are worth $150,000 today! His cars have appreciated so much he is embarrassed to talk about it. No doubt about it, inflation, affluence, increased demand and dwindling supply have convinced many enthusiasts that car collecting is a worthwhile investment. It is an argument that is used to justify the purchase of an old car to your wife, family and close friends. Unfortunately, it is only half true and for every great car that in time is worth two, three or four times its acquistion and restoration cost, there are five so-so cars that appreciate very slowly and are never worth even the cost of restoration (Fig. 4-1).

After locating and surveying over 60 professional restoration services in the United States and Canada, I found that most of them will restore only those cars which will be worth at least the cost of restoration when the work is completed. Aside from keeping the collector on the path of restoring desirable cars, this policy protects the shop from owning a worthless car in the event of nonpayment. It also puts their restorations to the forefront in any public display of old cars; the great ones always have the largest crowds around them.

Appreciation

How do you find out which cars are likely to appreciate most rapidly? Become active in one or more of the national clubs suited to your interests. Study the ads in the club magazines and in those specializing in offering old cars. Talk to experienced collectors at club meetings. Follow the prices paid in auctions and the prices asked in advertisements.

If you really love old cars, you should think carefully about the responsibilities of ownership before you tow that old wreck home. Unless you're a junk collector, you should have a heated garage (or one that can be heated) ready to house your new purchase. Be prepared to pay for the restoration out of surplus income. Some restoration shops, usually the larger ones, will agree to restore your car on a timetable geared to an amount you can pay each month.

Cost Factors

What does it cost to have professional restoration shop restore an old car? Plenty. The least expensive to restore are Fords. Some shops will fully restore a Model A Deluxe Roadster for as little as $20,000. The final price is based on the particular shop's hourly rate, plus materials. Wilkinson & Sharp (Feasterville, PA) estimates they can do a perfect brass radiator Model T for $25,000 to $35,000 (at a rate of $25 per hour plus materials) assuming no parts are missing and the wood and metal are still servicable. In all cases, a professional restoration shop will remove the body and start with the bare frame. About half the total cost will be for rebuilding the engine, gearbox, rearend, and frame. Do this mechanical work yourself and you can cut the cost about in half. The larger cars, like a Simplex or a Duesenberg will cost much more; $40,000 to $50,000 is not uncommon. A figure of $100,000 is possible with a large complex car such as a supercharged Duesenberg in "basket case" condition; i.e., boxes of parts that might become a car.

Restoration outside the United States or Canada is a possibility. The well-known lower labor rates are attractive and a number of American aficionados have shipped their cars abroad. In the case of Rolls-Royce and Bentley cars, this can be advantageous as Rolls-Royce will restore cars at the premises of their coachbuilding subsidiary, Park Ward, H.J. Mulliner, Ltd., and the level of their workmanship is extraordinary. The total cost will be not much less than the same work here but the quality, particularly in woodwork, will be superior.

The disadvantages of restoration abroad are numerous. Aside from Great Britain there is a language problem. The great distance involved will discourage mutual understanding on important details. Authenticity will be a problem as the Europeans don't really understand our requirements for show purposes. Any savings are usually offset by the cost of shipment both ways and insurance for the period involved.

A "cheap" restoration here or abroad is not possible. There are no magic short cuts! Potential customers looking for an inexpensive job are shown the door by any reputable restoration shop.

Are there legitimate ways of saving money on a professional restoration? Yes. Buy an unrestored car that is original, complete and with all woodwork and metal in usable condition. If you don't know dry rot from a dry Martini, take an expert with you. Without X-ray vision you won't avoid all the booby traps but you will beat most of them. If parts are missing, find them yourself and don't deliver the car for restoration until all the parts are in hand. Time you spend on chasing parts will simply lower the total cost by the number of hours involved.

Fig. 4-1. A less safe investment! A professionally restored 1938 Delahaye 135MS Roadster with exotic custom coachwork by Figoni and Falaschi of Paris. Its art deco style does not appeal to everyone. Courtesy Vintage Auto Restorations Inc., Ridgefield, CT.

Don't think you can achieve a direct saving by choosing the restoration shop with the lowest hourly rate. The hourly rate does not necessarily have anything to do with the final cost for a given car. A shop working slowly or inefficiently and charging a low rate will cost you more than a well-run shop charging more per hour. In all cases, you must judge by closely examining a completed example of the work of a particular shop.

Choosing a Shop

All of which brings us to the subject of how to choose the professional restoration shop for your particular car. Don't take the advice of the first enthusiastic friend whose 1910 Simplex was just beautifully restored by restoration shop "A." Your 1929 Packard will probably be done with less expense and greater authenticity by shop "B" where they know Packards intimately from long experience. Choose a shop experienced in your make of car.

Go to the club meets and talk to the owners of cars like your own. Be a good listener. Take notes. Carefully examine fully restored cars from the shops that have been recommended. Decide tentatively on one or two shops and call them for an appointment.

At this point, you are about to commit your prize possession for restoration and it is wise to approach these shops with the right mental attitude. Basically, very few of them need your business. Many are booked up two or three years ahead. If you call them on the phone, you will probably detect a tone of seeming reluctance to take on your project. Don't be put off. These shops have been conditioned by frequent phone calls from "bargain hunters." It will help if you mention the name of one of their steady customers. It will help even more if you will go to see them with photos of your car and a demonstrable understanding of the problems they will be facing in restoring your car.

Money must be discussed. It is most important that you have an understanding of how and when payments are to be made. While you're at the shop, look around and ask questions. It is usually wise to choose a shop with a methodical, well-organized approach to the problems inherent in reducing a complete automobile to 10,000 individual parts and putting them back together again (See Fig. 4-2). It is particularly important in a large shop restoring more than three or four cars at a time. At Vintage Auto Restorations Inc., Ridgefield, CT (specializing in Bugattis and vintage sports cars) and Hibernia Auto Restoration Inc., Hibernia, NJ, every car is photographed from all possible angles during each stage of dis-

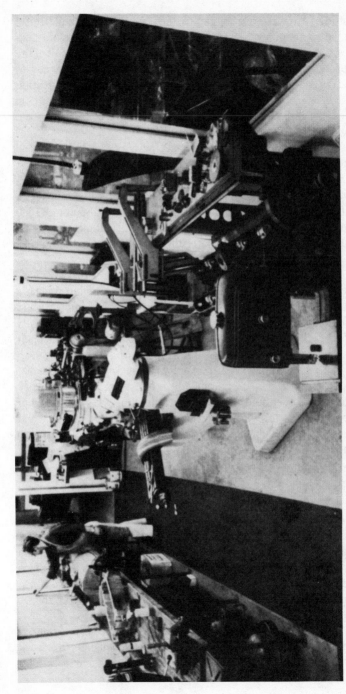

Fig. 4-2. A well organized fully equipped machine shop is a necessity for a professional restoration shop specializing in mechanical restoration work (courtesy of Vintage Auto Restorations Inc., Ridgefield, CT).

mantling. All parts are tagged as they are removed and stored together. Obviously, this saves much time and helps avoid mistakes when the car is put back together. Surprisingly, not all of the shops do this. Therefore, it is not naive to ask the owner to describe and show you the methods used to avoid misidentification and loss of parts. A certain amount of order should be apparent. On the other hand, national first prize winners have come from some rather grimy garages.

Part of the decision will depend on how you and the shop owner get along. If the chemistry is right, he'll agree to do the job and will accept a small deposit to put you "on the list." About a month before he's ready to accept the car, he will call you to make the final arrangements. Most shops will request a $500 to $1000 deposit to begin work (usually waived for old customers) and will want you to visit them soon after they receive the car to discuss various details.

A complete restoration can take six months to two years depending on what is involved. A bill is usually rendered once a month and if not paid promptly can result in stoppage of all work and commencement of storage charges or worse. If you have discussed the financial side of the transaction with the shop in a frank and open way, you will not face unexpected surprises.

For many enthusiasts, the ability to pay for the professional restoration of a favorite automobile is the culmination of every secret desire ever held. There is an exhilaration and satisfaction in every dollar spent to put every nut and bolt in its proper place and to see at least one object in this world brought close to perfection. When it's all over, he has the ultimate satisfaction. Utility. He can drive it home.

Do It Yourself

Without question, the overwhelming majority of old car restorations are done by the owners. To put it in another way, these cars are not restored by professional restoration shops. Few do-it-yourself restorers do every part of the job themselves, but they do take on the responsibility of being the prime contractor. This means all the work revolves around you and it also means a restoration completed at a final cost substantially lower than a professional shop would charge.

Cost savings is not the only motivation involved in deciding on the do-it-yourself route. There is the satisfaction of doing the work yourself, of mastering new skills, and of producing a prize winner with your own skill and knowledge (Fig. 4-3).

Fig. 4-3. A do-it-yourself Model A Ford restoration. The job is not perfect, but is perfectly wonderful for fun and (possible) profit. Owner: Ernest Swanson, Ridgefield, CT.

This does not mean that you will not use professional assistance. It is almost impossible to do every single job involved in a restoration yourself. If your time is limited you can confine yourself to dismantling and reassembling, farming out each part to the specialist needed to restore it and putting it back together when it is returned to you.

Consult Specialists When Needed

Even if you are anxious to do as much of the work as possible you cannot learn every skill required unless you plan to devote a lifetime to the restoration of one car. You will be limited by the amount of money you want to invest in tools. Even professional restoration shops send work out to specialists as it is simply uneconomical to employ specialists in every field required.

The remaining chapters of this book are based on the premise that you will be doing most of the work yourself or, at least, that you will be responsible for seeing that the work is done and done properly. This might be the case even if you are giving the car to a professional shop. Any work you can do or can be responsible for will reduce the bill and most restoration shops are delighted to work on this basis.

Your Time Is Money

A great deal of the time devoted to restoration is drudgery. Removing paint, wire brushing, sanding, cleaning, and polishing are typical examples. A professional restoration shop charges the same price for this work as they do for wiring, fitting, and assembling. If you do the drudge jobs you can save a great amount of money. Keep track of your hours and calculate the savings at $25 per hour.

Just as important is the time you will spend in locating missing parts. Time spent in this important pursuit can also be calculated as saving $25 per hour. Any restoration shop will charge you at approximately this rate for time devoted to "chasing parts."

Chapter 5
How To Begin

Begin with a place to work—where car and tools will remain undisturbed—and a camera. The first thing to do is photograph the car from every possible angle inside and out. Black and white film is fine as it is quicker and less expensive to have 8 by 10 enlargements made. Use a camera that will take quality pictures, at least a good 35mm or, better yet, a larger format camera such as a Rolleiflex. The idea is to produce enlargements that are sharp in every detail. Buy a book especially made to hold 8 by 10 prints under cellophane paper (try your local camera store or photography section of a department store.)

Photos Are Essential

A photographic record of the car before it is taken apart is important for, strangely enough, you will forget how it looked originally. Don't miss the details. Photograph all sides of the engine compartment, the hinges and locks of the hood and trunk and of each door. Don't forget the tops and bottoms of the doors when they are open as well as the top and bottom of the door sills. Pick a working area that is large enough to allow you to work on the body and chassis separately. An area the size of two cars is satisfactory. Be sure there is adequate artificial light as you can expect to work frequently at night. Check the electrical outlets and, if you're in a cold climate, be sure the place is heated or can be heated. With a valuable car and tools on hand you should be certain the building is secure. Paint the inside of the windows and nail up heavy screening on the inside. If the value of your car or cars is more than a few thousand dollars you would do well to look into the possibility of installing an alarm system.

A clean place to work is essential. Scrub the floor with soap and water and paint it light grey to make the dropped parts easier to find. While you're at it, paint the walls and ceiling the same light grey. It will brighten the room and you'll be more inclined to keep the shop clean.

Assemble Tools

A work bench, tools, and a place to store them, is desirable. Buy used ones through your local "buy-lines," "mart," or newspaper. Don't forget you will need metric tools if you are restoring a car made on the Continent of Europe or British Whitworth tools if the car was made in Great Britain. As a minimum you will need the following to get started:

3 screw drivers: straight edge—small, medium, large.
3 screw drivers: Phillips head—small, medium, large.
Full set of box end wrenches.
Full set of open end wrenches.
Full set of ½" or ⅜" socket wrenches with extension and ratchet bar.
2 Vice Grips: miniature and medium.
1 ballpeen hammer.
1 copper hammer.
1 cold chisel (to knock off bolt heads).
1 8" crescent wrench.
1 electric ⅜" variable speed drill.
1 standard set of high speed drill bits.
1 wire brush head to fit drill.
1 hacksaw with extra blades.
Wire brushes—soft and hard.
Scrapers—wide and narrow.
1 set of starter punches.
1 set of pin punches (to finish the job).

Don't skimp on tools. A full set of good tools will save you dozens of hours. Keep your hands and tools clean and always use the correct size for the job.

Take Notes

Keep a notebook on the car and its progress. An ordinary hard cover composition book is fine. Use this book for explanations and special notes that are not covered photographically. It will be especially useful to record solutions to parts problems and parts sources. Record keeping will save time in the long run.

Keep track of every penny you spend on the car. Make your entries in the back of the notebook. For a complete record show the date the purchase was made, whom it was paid to, include a description of what it was paid for, and the total amount. A complete financial record can be invaluable in proving how much you spent to a future purchaser or how little you spent—to your wife.

You will find the Yellow Pages of the telephone book extremely useful. Call the business office of your telephone company and request a copy of every Yellow Page directory for every city within 50 miles of your home (100 miles or more if you live far away from any big city.) These directories are usually available free on request.

The Art of Dismantling

What could be easier than taking apart a watch? And what could be more difficult than putting it together? Taking things apart, willy-nilly, can be terribly destructive and taking a car apart without following proper procedures will reduce its value to a fraction of its real worth. The correct method of dismantling is important and here is a list of some of the rules to be followed:

● Remove the battery!

● When removing nuts and bolts and washers to undo parts, always fasten the nut and bolt and washer back on to the removed part. If you are removing bolts from a panel and it is threaded, always screw the bolt back into the original thread. If you don't follow this procedure you will end up having coffee cans filled with nuts and bolts with no idea where they belong. If you must send some items out for plating, photograph them first and put them in a plastic bag tagged to indicate where they should go.

● Before you remove a part, photograph it, showing the surrounding area to indicate how it is installed. When you remove the part, place an identifying tag on it.

● As you remove parts which reveal other parts, photograph each step. Example: The inside of a door.

● As you remove any part from the car try to imagine yourself putting the same part back six months or a year later. Where an unusual number of steps are involved or where the order in which the items are installed is important, you must keep a record of the correct procedure in your notebook. In some cases, you may find that making drawings of the parts and accompanying notes are needed to reassemble them later. Photograph them also. The drawings and notes will simply explain the photographes. All this photographing and note-taking may seem tedious but you will find it invaluable later as you simply will not be able to remember every detail of the assembly when the time comes to put it all back together.

Bare the Chassis

If you are planning a thorough restoration which will result in a prize-winning car, you will want to remove the body and all other parts and start with a bare chassis. Most bodies are attached by six or eight bolts to the frame. Before you can take off the body you must remove the seats, floorboards, and steering column. Then, disconnect all lines running from the chassis to the body. These include:

Electric wires – when these are cut, wrap paper tape around each wire to form a tab and mark both ends you have just cut with a code letter or number. Use a different code for each cut.

Speedometer and tachometer (if any) cables, oil pressure line from engine to gauge, water temperature line from radiator to gauge, and lines to any other gauges your car may have.

If you have *hydraulic brakes,* drain all the fluid from the system and disconnect the line going from the master cylinder to the brake fluid reservoir tank.

If you have vacuum operated *windshield wipers* you need to remove the vacuum line from the engine.

Remove all fenders, running boards, trim panels on both sides of the engine compartment, radiator shell, and radiator. Photograph the area where the part has been removed, first circling the bolt lines with white chalk for future identification.

Make a further study of the body to be sure nothing more needs to be removed on your particular car. If you are working on a closed car, remove the doors. Check again to be sure you have located and removed all bolts holding the body to the frame.

Now you need four or five strong friends to help you. With two or three on either side it should be possible to lift off the body. If it does not come off, look for bolts you might have missed; otherwise, you may have a rust problem which has bonded the brackets together. Try soaking them in Liquid Wrench and giving each bracket a hard shot with the hammer. If all else fails, you may have to place four jacks under the body and slowly jack the body off the frame, or you may have overlooked some bolts.

With the body off, the chassis should be photographed from all angles before further dismantling takes place. Next, remove the engine, gearbox, and drive shaft separately. Do not proceed further without a Workshop Manual for your car. These are available for most makes and usually give detailed instructions for removal of the rear axle springs, and other suspension parts.

Remove the gas tank and inspect the inside for rust. Even a small amount of rust here can clog fuel lines and flood the carburetors. To remove any rust fill the tank with just enough gravel to cover the bottom. Now find a friend to help you and shake the tank vigorously in all directions. Wash out with water and repeat. When all the rust is removed, let the tank dry and use a fuel tank slushing compound. (We suggest Pro Tech, manufactured by Pro Tech Products Co., 8846 Alondra Blvd., Bellflower, CA 90706.) Fill the tank with the slushing compound as directed, tape all holes and rotate the tank in all directions. Blow out the pickup tube after an hour or two and let dry for 24 hours. The tank is now sealed with a rubberlike skin.

By this time the frame should be resting on saw horses or jack stands and you can now remove everything from the frame that is removable. Don't forget to photograph the frame at each stage of removal and tag each part describing its position in the car.

Now that you have the car completely dismantled, spread on the floor all around you, it is wise to take an hour or two to decide just how much of this work you want to do yourself. You may be discouraged at the tremendous number of parts that make up a complete automobile. Now is the time to decide which jobs require specialized knowledge which you do not possess and do not wish to acquire.

Engine, Transmission and Rear Axle

These are among the largest and most important parts of the car and do require very special skills, knowledge, and experience to rebuild. If you are restoring a Ford you might ask the service manager at your local Ford dealer if any of the older mechanics might be interested in taking on your job on his own time at his house. Regardless of make, you will get the best job done at the lowest price by seeking out a shop or individual mechanic with direct experience in your particular make of car. If you own a very rare car, such as a Bugatti, it is particularly important to entrust it only to a shop specializing in that type of car.

Most professional restoration shops are delighted to carry out a rebuild on your running gear and many of these are able to run the engines before returning them to you. If the shop is not too far away, you will probably prefer to tow the chassis to them, when it is completed, and let them install the engine (and other components) before it is started for the first time.

If you should decide to rebuild the engine and the rest of the running gear yourself, you should obtain a workshop manual and the advice and assistance of an experienced mechanic.

Brakes

Bring your brake drums and brake shoes to a local brake shop (look under "Brake Service" in your telephone book Yellow Pages). They will check the inside of the drums for out-of-round wear and will skim them off, if needed, to bring the back to true round. The brake shoes will be lined with new material. A soft lining material is recommended if your car has mechanical brakes or hydraulic brakes with no booster, i.e., without power assist. The softer lining will result in lower pedal pressure and a more progressive braking effect that is easier to control.

Brake fluid is a very effective but expensive paint remover. To avoid any possibility of ruining an expensive paint job you should investigate the newly developed silicone brake fluid which is inert and has no effect on any type of paint. (Contact the Marketing Supervisor, Mechanical Fluids, Dow Corning Corp., Midland, Michigan 48640.) A further benefit of silicone brake fluid is the fact that it does not attract and absorb water as ordinary brake fluid does. This feature alone makes it ideal for old cars whose brake lines, wheel cylinders, and master cylinders are particularly susceptible to corrosion.

Suspension

Springs that are sagging or broken should be replaced. If the springs are sagging you will have to check the workshop manual for the original specifications: take your springs and specifications to your local automotive spring specialist (see Yellow Pages in your telephone book under "Springs-Automotive-Sales and Service").

Kingpins and bushings should be examined and replaced if excessively worn.

The front spindles, the shafts which hold the brakes and wheels, should be magnafluxed to detect cracks in the metal which might cause the spindle to break. Usually, the local "hot rod" or racing shop will know where the nearest magnaflux service is located. (See your telephone book Yellow Pages under "Automobile Racing and Sports Car Equipment.")

Steering

The steering arm should also be magnafluxed. This is the large part which controls the tie rods and is attached directly to the shaft coming out of the steering box.

An old car which steers badly is unpleasant to drive and is a danger on the roads. Carefully examine every part of the entire steering mechanism and replace all worn or broken parts. The key to good steering is the steering box itself. Take it apart completely and replace all worn bushings and parts that are defective or broken (see your workshop manual for detailed instructions on dismantling, reassembly, and final adjustment to eliminate "play"). Replace worn tie rod ends and ball joints. If you replace or rebuild every worn part from the steering wheel to the front wheels, and if it is all properly adjusted, you will enjoy steering equal to or better than that which the car possessed when new.

Chapter 6
Dealing With
Corrosion, Grime and Paint

Will Coca-Cola remove rust? Yes, it will and it's worth remembering in a pinch but most uneconomical for any extended use. Take the frame and other large, heavy steel pieces to a sandblasting shop, *after* they have been cleaned with gunk or by steam cleaning. Parts that are excessively dirty and greasy *are* best cleaned by steam cleaning. Professional steam cleaning units can be rented from many large hardware stores. (See "Steam Cleaning Equipment" in your telephone book Yellow Pages.) The sandblasting will remove all rust and paint and all other foreign matter. Do not sandblast any body panels, or any lightweight panels. As soon as the parts are returned from the sandblasters, wash them down with paint thinner to remove all dust, wait for it to dry and paint them with a good enamel or lacquer primer. Fill any corroded areas with "body filler" available from any automotive paint shop. An unusual product that removes rust without sandblasting and creates its own primer surface is *OSPHO* made by Skybryte Co., 3125 Perkins Ave., Cleveland, Ohio 44114. Ospho painted on a rusted surface that has been wire brushed will turn the iron oxide into iron phosphate, an inert substance that turns the metal black after a white residue is brushed off.

Smaller parts can be derusted and stripped by leaving them for a few hours in a diluted solution of sulphuric acid. A much safer method is to use PF-47 chemical rust remover (See Appendix C).

Paint Removal

Removing paint from large or small sheet metal panels can be handled in several ways. If you don't want to do it yourself, try taking the pieces to your local furniture stripper. Their equipment is usually large enough to handle items as large as fenders and doors. For the main structure of the body, you will have to use commercial paint remover (purchased by the gallon from your local paint or hardware store). This is hard work and is best done outdoors.

The sun will accelerate the process and the foul smell will be blown away. Follow the directions on the can, wear gloves, and move the paint off with wire brushes and steel wool. Wash thoroughly with water and let dry. Then wash again with paint thinner and let dry. Finally, go over all surfaces with a blow torch. Be careful not to heat the metal so that it cannot be touched. Overheating will cause the metal to distort. All of these final steps are to eliminate foreign matter which can cause the paint to "lift."

In recent years, a specialized business has come into being and it uses huge tanks which are large enough to lower a complete automobile body into. These companies specialize in removing paint and rust using special chemicals and these are perfectly compatible with all steel bodies or all aluminum bodies. These companies are listed every month in large ads in *Hemming's Motor News* and *Cars and Parts*. A complete list of these companies is found under Paint Removal in Appendix B.

If a fender or other panel is rusted or corroded beyond repair, you will be facing a tough or easy problem, depending on the type of car involved. Pre-war Ford fenders and most other Ford body parts are available from firms specializing in Ford parts. Fenders for post-war American cars are available from junk yards or through other collectors and clubs specializing in that make of car. Body parts for very rare and limited production cars such as Rolls-Royce and Duesenberg must be *made*.

Coachbuilding

Coachbuilding, the fabricating of complete automobile bodies in metal involving compound curves, is an almost extinct art in the United States. Only a handful of the shops, listed in Appendix A, are capable of producing a complete automobile body and only a few more can make a fender or door (Fig. 6-1). Call the restoration shops nearest to you. If they cannot do the job themselves, they will probably be able to refer you to a shop where they can.

Fabricating Parts

Metal fabricating that does not involve compound curves is easier to cope with (See Figs. 6-2 and 6-3). If nearby restoration

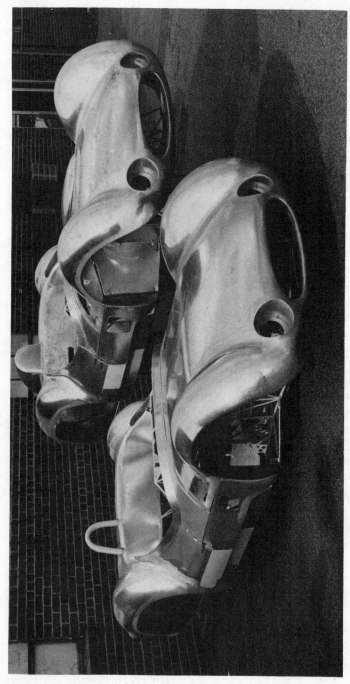

Fig. 6-1. Two new Maserati Birdcage bodies fabricated from aluminum by Grand Prix SSR Co., E. Setauket, NY.

Fig. 6-2. A new radiator shell for a Ford racer made by metal fabrication specialists (courtesy of Chester Auto Restoration Service, Chester, NJ).

shops are not able to assist you, try the Yellow Pages of your telephone book under "Assembly and Fabricating," "Metal Stamping" and "Tanks-Metal."

Traditional preference among old car lovers and professional restorers is still for the original pre-war type of lacquer and it is used in the great majority of fine restorations despite its tendency to crack with age. Aluminum bodied cars are especially prone to paint cracking because aluminum expands and contracts to a greater degree than steel. The lacquer does not expand and contract to the same degree and cracking will eventually result at stress points such as at the corners of the trunk lid where a narrow radius exists.

Automotive "Paints"

Enamel expands and contracts more than lacquer. It is generally more flexible and is, therefore, much less prone to cracking. Unfortunately, it is difficult to apply enamel to achieve a perfect result and it is usually too soft to smooth out by the use of fine rubbing compounds such as would be used on a lacquer surface.

The newer acrylic automotive paints are worth serious consideration for their special qualities. Acrylic enamel is ideal for use on aluminum bodied cars as it expands and contracts like ordinary enamel, but is much harder and can be rubbed out after allowing a month or two to harden. An ideal acrylic enamel for the beginner to try is DuPont Centari. It dries in air in 20 to 30 minutes provided the humidity in the air is low. Use it with a compatible primer and follow the directions carefully.

Acrylic lacquer will produce a superb glass-like finish, but it is known to be very hard and difficult to rub out with compound.

Fig. 6-3. A new rocker panel fabricated from sheet steel for the restoration of a Jaguar XK120 (courtesy of Grand Prix SSR Co., E. Setauket NY).

However, hard work will produce outstanding results and there is every indication that acrylic lacquer will far outlast the ordinary lacquer.

Whatever you use, be sure that the filler, the primer coat, and the finish coats are compatible (See Figs. 6-4 and 6-5). The use of an enamel primer with a lacquer finish, for example, will result in the lacquer "lifting" off the surface. Also, for best results, do not paint on days of high humidity or extremely high heat (over 85 degrees Fahrenheit).

Striping

Striping machines are available from large hardware stores and art supply stores, but the results they produce are disappointing. The professionals do their striping "free-hand" but unless you have an aptitude for this art you should find a professional to do it for you. If you cannot locate a professional through the members of your car club, try the nearest "hot rod/custom car shop." Striping has become a very popular form of decoration for those types of cars. Also, many sign painters can stripe cars and these can be easily found in the telephone book Yellow Pages.

For post-war cars, try the newly developed clear tape stripes which are applied like cellophane tape. These stripes are available

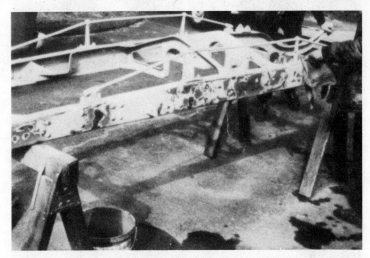

Fig. 6-4. A better than new professionally painted chassis will be achieved by filling all the low spots with "filler" after the primer has been applied (courtesy of Vintage Auto Restorations, Inc. Ridgefield, CT).

Fig. 6-5. A completed chassis that has been professionally restored to better than new condition. Note the reflections on the side of the frame (courtesy of Vintage Auto Restorations Inc., Ridgefield, CT).

in various widths and colors and are quite convincing if you don't examine the surface of the car too closely. (See under "Automobile Parts and Supplies — Retail" in your telephone book Yellow Pages.)

Chapter 7
Finding Wheels And Tires

You might find it less expensive to buy new or rebuilt wheels, road or steering, rather than attempt restoration. See Appendix C for a full list of parts suppliers and wheel restorers.

Road Wheels

Wooden wheels are being made new and repaired by professional wheelwrights. Minor repairs can be handled by a local cabinet maker if you can talk him into it.

Metal disc wheels can be repaired and straightened by a wheel shop in the nearest big city. See "Wheels" in your telephone book Yellow Pages.

Wire wheels that are out of round, rusted, cracked, or have broken spokes, must be rebuilt. They must be completely taken apart, sandblasted and made perfectly round with new spokes as required, painted or chrome plated, and balanced (See Fig. 7-1). Wire wheels are a specialty and unless a local service exists to tackle your wheels I recommend that you have the work done by Dayton Wheel Products Inc., 2326 E. River Road, Dayton, Ohio 45439. To find a possible local shop, call your nearest M.G., Triumph, or Jaguar new car dealer's service manager.

Steering Wheels

Over the years, steering wheels have been made in a wide variety of materials (Fig. 7-2). Most use a center core of steel or aluminum which is then covered in hard rubber, wood or plastic. All of these types are restored by Bill Peters Restorations, 37 DeKoven Court, Brooklyn, New York 11230, telephone 212-434-7721.

Wooden steering wheels are the specialty of Mark Wallach Ltd., 27 New St., Nyack, New York 10960, telephone 914-358-8179. Mark is a master craftsman who can reproduce a wooden steering wheel with all new materials or repair your original steering wheel provided it is in reasonably good condition.

Tires

What was once a difficult replacement job has been made easy by the tremendous demand created by the ever-increasing number of hobbyists. If the size of your tire was very popular, you will find a wide variety of makes and styles available (see Appendix C). If the size you require is not available commercially, advertise for it in a magazine such as *Hemming's* or *Old Cars* (see Appendix C).

The new "old tires and tubes" made now are using modern materials and have all but eliminated the memorable and frequent "blowouts" of the past. This is one part of automotive history we do not want to preserve.

Fig. 7-1. A wire wheel in primer after being returned from a specialist rebuilding service (courtesy of Vintage Auto Restorations Inc., Ridgefield, CT).

Fig. 7-2. An original Model A Ford steering wheel. Owner: Ernest Swanson, Ridgefield, CT.

Check your owner's manual and be sure to buy the tire size used on your car originally. Do not be tempted by oversized tires that might fit your rims. They will make your car look "tire heavy" and will put a strain on the steering and other running gear it was not originally designed for.

Chapter 8
Platers and Polishers

Some years ago I visited one of the best professional restoration shops in Los Angeles. The owner and I chatted as he prepared a shipment of small parts in a heavy crate. I guessed that these were parts to be chrome plated and I inquired as to why they were being crated. The answer was that all of his plating was done in San Francisco despite the fact that there were over a dozen platers in the Los Angeles area.

The problem is that most platers are not very interested in restoration work and are not sympathetic to the needs of the restorer. Unfortunately, a great many of the items that require plating are badly worn and/or require repairs which most platers cannot cope with (See Fig. 8-1). Commercial platers build their business on job lot work that usually consists of plating new parts for a manufacturer on a contract basis. The plating of old worn pieces on an individual basis is usually done as an "accommodation," often with the implication that they are doing you a favor.

Restoring and Repairing

A new development is the plater who is specializing in restoration work and who is willing to do some repair work (See Appendix C). If one of those shops is not near you and you don't want to do business by mail you might try locating a plater who specializes in marine hardware. (See under "Plating" in your telephone book Yellow Pages.)

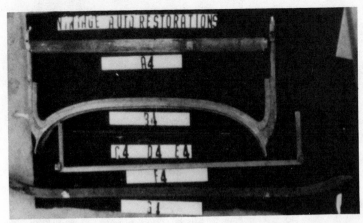

Fig. 8-1. A record photo made of windshield hardware before the pieces are sent to the platers. A list of the items is also made, matching the photo, and a copy is given to the plater to serve as an inventory (courtesy of Vintage Auto Restorations Inc., Ridgefield, CT).

Repairs to items made of copper, brass, or aluminum can usually be made by a local silversmith or, for smaller parts—even a jeweler.

Finding someone to repair pitted or damaged zinc die castings is even more difficult. One expert in this specialty is Milestone Car Society member Bill Parmenter, 5502 28th Parkway, Hillcrest Heights, MD 20031, who is setting up a service to help restorers. Alternatively, discuss your problem pieces with the most cooperative plater you can find.

Polishing

Platers are also professional polishers. Before the plating can begin, the item must be thoroughly cleaned and highly polished. Thus, polishing can be destructive unless the operator is very careful! See Fig. 8-2. Thin pieces can be polished through until they disappear. The detail work cast or engraved in a trim piece or sculptured mascot can be polished away. On delicate items like this, the plater must be warned to keep his polishing to a minimum.

Polishing of brass lamps and other brightwork is best done the hard way, by hand. Use a good polish such as Brasso and keep the items covered as much as possible to inhibit oxidation.

Demand Quality Work

Inferior plating is useless. All plating on an old car is subject to close scrunity. Let the plater know that you expect a quality job and

Fig. 8-2. This Model A Ford mascot's beauty is due, in large measure, to the fine details in the bird's head, tail and wings. A plater who is not very careful can polish these details away, greatly reducing the beauty and value of the mascot. Owner: Ernest Swanson, Ridgefield, CT.

that any piece which later blisters or flakes off will be required to be redone properly. Quality plating means plating first with copper, next with nickel and, finally, with chrome. Similar steps are taken with nickel plating, which was the correct finish before chrome came into general use in the 1930s.

Inspect the Job

When you pick up work from the plater's be sure to inspect it carefully and immediately return any pieces which show signs of blistering or flaking. Also, watch for areas which have not been fully plated. Sometimes these are deep within a cavity or in a severely under-cut area and the plater might not be able to do any better without special equipment.

Threaded parts (screws, bolts, and studs) that are plated will usually not fit back into their original threaded place (nut or other topped piece) due to the additional thickness of the plating. To avoid this problem, ask your plater to mask these parts. If he charges extra for this, you can mask them yourself with sealing wax or black plastic electical tape.

Plating wire or small springs will cause them to become brittle. Heat treating will be required to offset this. If your plater does not know what to do, get advice from a heat treating expert. Look under "Heat Treating—Metal" in your telephone book Yellow Pages.

Some other forms of plating which can be useful in restoration work can also be recommended:

- Cadmium—ideal for rustproofing nuts and bolts.
- Soft Chrome—The result is a satin finish not unlike hand polished steel. The finish is sometimes used for front axles, tie rods, and steering arms.

Chapter 9
Woodwork And Springs

Woodwork problems fall into three categories: 1) reproduction of wooden parts destroyed by rot or termites; 2) restoration of wooden parts that have deteriorated badly and may also be partially destroyed; and 3) refinishing of metal parts that were originally wood-grained. The first and last require special equipment and skill but the second one is easy to learn and refinishing kits giving excellent results are available in any hardware store.

Reproduction of Wooden Parts

There are services available to the automotive hobbyist for copying wooden pieces using your old piece as a pattern (see Appendix C and Fig. 9-1). Your local cabinet maker (see under "Cabinet Maker" in your telephone book Yellow Pages) is also capable of reproducing these wooden pieces if you can talk him into doing it. Again, a visit in a fellow club member's fully restored old car may get him interested enough to help you. Some wood parts are available immediately from the parts supplier who specializes in your make.

Restoration of Wooden Parts

Refinishing of decorative wood pieces can be accomplished quite easily using materials available in any paint or hardware store. Definitive refinishing instructions can be found in numerous books available in the library. If that's too much trouble, buy a

Fig. 9-1. New wood framing of seasoned ash and plywood, duplicating the original, for a 1938 Rolls-Royce (courtesy of Grand Prix SSR Co., E. Setauket, NY).

refinishing kit—also available in paint and hardware stores—and follow the directions to the letter.

Dry Rot in Wood

The bodies of many of the more expensive luxury cars of the pre-World War II and early post-war period were made with hardwood framing to which the aluminum or steel panels were attached. If the wood framing is rotted, you will have to have it all replaced. If it is rotted, test the wood by inserting the sharp end of a pen knife blade into the wood (with the grain—not across the grain). If the wood is "as new" it will take a great deal of effort to insert the knife. If the knife goes in easily, but the wood is otherwise not rotted, the wood can probably be saved by drilling holes ½" apart to 80 percent of the depth of the wood and pouring in "Git-Rot" (marketed by Boat Life, Hicksville, NY 11801 through

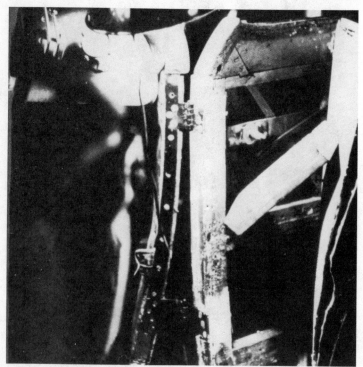

Fig. 9-2. A good example of a record shot showing the construction of a wood framed door and how blocks of wood were carefully pieced into the door frame to provide strong new wood for the hinge screws (courtesy of Vintage Auto Restorations Inc., Ridgefield, CT).

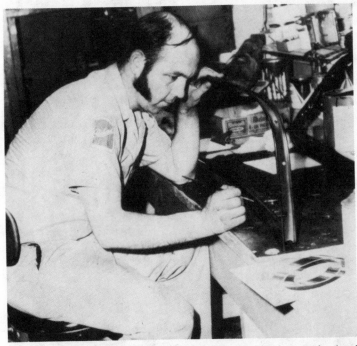

Fig. 9-3. Woodgraining applied by hand to a window molding by a professional (courtesy of Hibernia Auto Restorations, Inc. Hibernia, NJ).

most boatyards and boat dealers). Follow the directions carefully. This is a plastic substance that is mixed from two different cans. This substance will restore the strength of dry rotted wood provided the wood is not rotted so badly that it is falling apart. It is particularly important to use this treatment where door hinges are screwed into the wood and at joints where two pieces of wood are joined (See Fig. 9-2).

Restoration of Woodgrained Metal Parts

Kits are available and you can learn to do this yourself. At slight additional cost and great reduction in frustration we recommend having woodgraining done professionally (see Appendix C and Fig. 9-3).

Springs: Large and Small

Large coil springs and leaf springs used for the suspension of a car are available from the nearest automotive spring shop (see "Springs—Automotive—Sales and Service" in your telephone

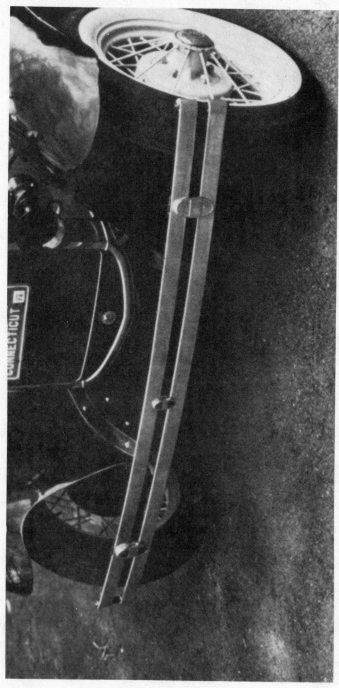

Fig. 9-4. This chrome plated spring steel bumper for a Model A Ford is available from Ford parts specialists, but this type of bumper can be made by an automotive springs shop. **Owner:** Ernest Swanson, Ridgefield, CT.

Fig. 9-5. With dimensioned drawings, or from an old set of original springs, an automotive spring shop can duplicate this quarter-elliptic spring from a Type 51A Bugatti (courtesy of Vintage Auto Restorations, Inc. Ridgefield, CT).

book Yellow Pages). If the original specifications for the springs are available, bring them along with the springs from the car. Final adjustment shiming or re-arching, cannot be done until the car is completely reassembled with all of its weight again on the chassis. See Fig. 9-4.

Small springs are available in almost infinite variety from a spring supply house (see "Springs—Coil, flat, etc.—Distrs. and Mfrs." in your telephone book Yellow Pages). Special springs can be made to order (Fig. 9-5). The usual minimum order is one to two dozen so you may want to pool your with other members to make it worthwhile. Be sure to bring a sample and make it clear that you want precisely the same design. Also, be sure to specify that the diameter and strength of the wire must be the same as the sample.

If small springs must be chrome plated, be sure they are heat treated to take away the brittleness (see Chapter 8).

Chapter 10
Metal and Machined Parts

Large, hollow, symmetrical pieces, e.g., headlight rims and shells, are easily reproduced by a process known as metal spinning (See Fig. 10-1). In metal spinning, a thin sheet of steel, aluminum, copper, or brass is shaped over a wooden mold that is the exact shape and size of the piece you want to reproduce.

Obtaining Spun-Metal Parts

First, locate a metal spinner. This could be a small local company in the metal spinning business (see under "Metal Spinning" in the telephone book Yellow Pages), or the metal working teacher in the local high school. A company might require a minimum order of a dozen or more. In this case, spread the word in your car club and take orders for the extra pieces you can't use.

Cast Metal Parts

Any cast-metal part can be reproduced by a foundry. (See Figs. 10-2 through 10-5). Small foundries usually work aluminum, brass, and bronze alloys. In most cases, only larger foundries will cast iron or steel and they are usually not interested in doing small jobs for hobbyists. Don't worry. There are dozens of items you can have made easily and inexpensively by a small foundry. A partial list: door handles (inside and out), window winding handles, metal knobs, metal pull handles, mascots, hub covers, engine mounts, valve covers, and water jacket plates. See "Foundries" in your telephone book Yellow Pages.

Fig. 10-1. This headlight shell can be made by the metal spinning process. The smaller parts would be added later by a metal fabricator (courtesy of Vintage Auto Restorations Inc., Ridgefield, CT).

Aluminum Reproduces Smaller

If you give an original piece to the foundry to use as their pattern, the copies will be slightly smaller, about 3/16" per foot less for aluminum, which shrinks less than bronze or brass. If this is important you can have the original piece cast in expansion plater which will grow larger to compensate for the shrinkage. This involves an extra step and will increase the cost.

Make a Wood Pattern

The only alternative would be to make a model of the piece out of hard wood (usually called a pattern) slightly larger than required. Professional pattern makers can be contacted through a foundry but are usually quite expensive so you might try to find a cabinet maker or hobbyist with a woodworking shop to make it for you. Don't forget, once you have the pattern (or a spare original) you can easily have more pieces made by the foundry and offer them to others in the hobby who may have the same problem. Most foundries will trim off the excess metal. Some further finishing and machining may be required and you should find out if this is included in the quoted price.

Rubber Mold Reproductions

Small metal parts can also be reproduced by a rubber mold process utilizing a low temperature metal alloy. The rubber mold cannot be used more than a dozen times but this is probably not important for the pieces you need to have reproduced (see "Foundries" in your telephone book Yellow Pages).

"Lost-Wax" Method

Small metal parts can also be reproduced by the "lost-wax" method used by jewelers and dental laboratories. It is usually

Fig. 10-2. A bronze casting (made by a foundry from a wood pattern) is used to lower the front of the frame of a Model T Ford-based racer. On the right of the photo it is as it comes from the foundry. At left, it is shown after the face has been machined and drilled. Owner: Robert Swanson, Ridgefield, CT.

Fig. 10-3. This particular Model A Ford door handle is a reproduction available from Ford parts specialists. It could also be reproduced by a foundry. Owner: Ernest Swanson, Ridgefield, CT.

Fig. 10-4. This unusual mascot, picked up at a flea market, could be reproduced by a foundry, although the quality of the details would be improved by using the rubber mold or lost wax method. Owner: Ernest Swanson, Ridgefield, CT.

Fig. 10-5. A Ford Model A rumble seat step plate which could be made by a machine shop if it were not available from a Ford parts specialist. Owner: Ernest Swanson, Ridgefield, CT.

Fig. 10-6. This knurled knob is a typical machine shop item which can be very expensive if only one is made or quite inexpensive if made in quantity. Owner: Ernest Swanson, Ridgefield, CT.

considered too expensive for hobbyists unless you can learn the method in an arts and crafts school and do it at home.

Machined Parts

Small fully-machined parts can be reproduced from the original or from drawings by any competent machinist. (See Figs. 10-5 and 10-6). Here again, the problem is to find the right machinist and/or the right machine shop (see "Automobile Machine Shop Service" and "Machine Shops" in your telephone book Yellow Pages). You might also try finding a part-time or retired machinist by advertising in the local help-wanted columns.

Chapter 11

Glass, Plexiglas and Plastics

Glass parts cannot be reproduced economically in small quantities. Many glass parts are available commercially, "NOS" or reproductions, and a thorough search of these sources is advised before you investigate the possibility of making new parts.

Minimum Orders

Any commercial glass company will want a minimum order of 500 to 1000 pieces representing a sizable investment. If your club is interested in such a project, look for a likely glass company in the telephone book Yellow Pages of the nearest large city under the section "Glassware—Whol. & Mfrs."

Using Plastics

Small glass pieces can be reproduced with convincing results in clear or colored plastic (See Fig. 11-1). Only close examination will reveal they are not real glass. This method or reproduction is done by the rubber mold method. Small plastic pieces can be reproduced the same way. See "Plastics—Molders" in the telephone book Yellow Pages.

Safety Glass

Flat safety glass for windshields, side, and rear windows is easily obtained from your local automotive glass shop. See "Glass—Automobile, Plate, Window, Etc.—Dealers" in your

Fig. 11-1. Small lenses that were originally made in glass can be economically reproduced in small quantities in plastic by the rubber mold method. Owner: Ernest Swanson, Ridgefield, CT.

telephone book Yellow Pages. When having windshield glass replaced, be sure state inspection laws are met. In most states, the glass must be specially marked to show it is approved safety glass.

Curved safety glass for the windshield is more difficult. Owners of old Ferrari's have located several sources for custom made curved safety glass and I suggest you write to both the Ferrari Owner's Club and the Ferrari Club of America (See Appendix B) for the latest information on this subject.

Plexiglas

For curved rear windows or side windows, install Plexiglas. Specialists in bending and installing Plexiglas can usually be found through automobile racing shops and also at airport shops specializing in airplane and helicopter interiors. Or you can try cutting, forming, and fitting it yourself. Suggestions are available from Plexiglas suppliers found under "Plastics—Rods, Tubes, Sheets, Etc.—Supply Centers" in the telephone book Yellow Pages.

Chapter 12

Welding and Metal Stitching

Using the techniques of industry in the area of "cold welding," hot welding and metal stitching, it is possible to repair almost anything that has been broken. Even in cases of an engine destroying itself by "throwing a rod" it is usually possible to repair the engine to its original running condition. Every restoration shop which does engine work must know the techniques in current use and have the ability to carry out these repairs themselves or have experience with specialists who can be trusted.

Heli-Arc Welding

The welding of large aluminum castings such as cylinder heads is probably the most difficult repair to effect with 100 percent success. Welding aluminum can cause it to distort so it will no longer fit the piece it is to be mated to. The answer is Heli-Arc welding, (Fig. 12-1), a low temperature gas weld in an atmosphere of helium. Using this method an experienced operator can make the repair with no measurable distortion.

Acetylene Gas Welding

Acetylene gas welding can be used to repair successfully iron blocks and other cast iron pieces and distortion will not be measurable provided the area to be welded is not too large.

Fig. 12-1. Heli-arcing new aluminum panels for a Jaguar XK120 door (courtesy of Grand Prix SSR Co., E. Setauket, NY).

Fig. 12-2. An excellent example of metal stitching. In this case, a hole in the side of an engine block is replaced with a steel plate that is stitched to the block by the use of interlocking threaded brass plugs. This is a "cold" process which precludes the possibility of distortion (courtesy of Vintage Auto Restorations Inc., Ridgefield, CT).

A Cold Method

For large areas, metal stitching is much less risky (Fig. 12-2). This method is completely cold. Holes are drilled between the original block and the repair plate. The holes are tapped and brass plugs threaded in so they overlap and interlock. This method guarantees no distortion.

If distortion does occur in a piece that has been welded, it can be corrected by remachining one or more of the surfaces.

This is expensive but not a total disaster.

Chapter 13

Instruments and the Electrical System

The restoration of instruments can require four separate operations:

● The nickel or chrome plating, or polishing, or painting of the rim surrounding the face.

● Renewing of the face. In some cases only careful cleaning is required. In others, the face is so faded or chipped or discolored that it is hardly legible and a new face must be made exactly duplicating the original.

● The instrument works should be sent out to a competent instrument repair man even if you know the instrument is working properly. This is done to be sure the instrument is clean, properly lubricated, that all connections are tight, and that no part is so worn that it is about to fail (See Fig. 13-1).

● The back of the case must be derusted and cleaned and painted.

Several services are listed in Appendix C which will take care of all these areas and return the instrument to you in "as new" condition (Fig. 13-2).

Restorations

If you want to handle these operations separately, do not take the instrument apart. Simply clean the outside thoroughly and send it first to an instrument repair service (see Appendix C). When it is

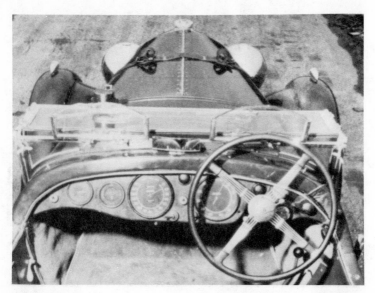

Fig. 13-1. This full set of original instruments on a 1928 Bentley 4½-litre LeMans Tourer are in very good original condition and are preferable to a new reproduction.

returned you can simply paint the back, send the rim to the plater, and the face to a service specializing in this type of work.

If the indicator needle does not come off easily, take it to your nearest watch repair man. He will be able to remove it correctly with his special tools. If necessary, remove the paint from the needle and repaint it with a thin coat of black lacquer applied with a fine brush.

Making new faces is part of the normal business of restoring old clocks. Look for a shop near you that sells or restores old clocks. They will do the job for you or will be able to refer you to a special service.

Using New or Rebuilt Parts

If you find that new or rebuilt instruments are available from one of the parts suppliers (see Appendix C) you might save money by buying them rather than having them restored.

Electrical System

Start with a new battery of the proper size. As you will not use the car every day buy a quality battery that will more likely hold its charge for long periods. Also, buy a new ground wire (from the battery to the chassis) and a new "hot cable" (from the battery to the starter motor).

Use the Correct Wiring Diagram

A wiring diagram is essential in order to allow duplication of the original electrical system and to enable you to double check your work. Look at the wiring diagram to find out if your system is "positive ground" or "negative ground." If the diagram indicates the ground wire goes from the + (plus) terminal of the battery, you have a positive ground system. If the ground wire goes from the − (minus) terminal, you have a negative ground system. Most old American and English cars are "positive ground" and most old French, German, Swedish, and Italian cars are "negative ground."

Starter Motor and Generator

Send your starter motor and generator out to be checked and rebuilt as necessary (See "Automobile Electric Service" in your telephone book Yellow Pages.) Paint them when they are returned, being careful not to get the paint into the insides. Also, have them check your voltage regulator. If any of these units require major

Fig. 13-2. Every detail of this 1938 Delahaye instrument panel has been professionally restored (courtesy of Vintage Auto Restorations Inc., Ridgefield, CT).

repairs you may find it cheaper to buy new or rebuilt units from one of the parts suppliers specializing in your type of car.

Replacing every wire in your car can be a tedious and time-consuming project. Fortunately, complete wiring harnesses (all of the wires correctly assembled and wrapped for installation exactly as they were installed by the factory) are available for many of the most popular cars (see Appendix C).

Check Electrical Connections

Check the electrical connections of all the tail lights, head lights, parking lights, brake lights, instrument lights, and interior lights. If any connection is broken and you cannot repair it, try taking it to your local "fixit" man who repairs toasters, waffle irons, etc.

To learn the basic principles of electricity and of your automotive electrical system consult your local library and the book sellers listed in Appendix C.

Chapter 14
Upholstery

Under the broad category of upholstery are seats, headlining, doors, carpet, tops, top boots (tonneau covers), wheel covers, and anything that is made of cloth, leather, or material of any kind.

If your wife or a good friend is a competent seamstress, you might be able to get all the upholstery done at a very low cost. However, a normal sewing machine cannot be used to sew upholstery. A heavy duty machine made expressly for heavy materials is required. Books on automotive upholstery are available and will be a great help (see Appendix C). Unless you expect to restore a good many cars you will find it less costly to have the work done by an upholsterer than to invest in a heavy duty sewing machine.

Try a Kit!

For the most popular cars, Fords, M.G.'s, and many others, the favorite solution is the use of upholstery kits (Figs. 14-1 and 14-2). Most of these kits are of high quality, using the correct original materials. They are easy to install and give a most professional result. Upholstery kits are available for seats, headlinings, tops, panels and trim, side curtains, and top boots (tonneau covers). See Appendix C.

. . . Or Use A Professional

For the very best work, use a professional upholsterer (Fig. 14-3) who specializes in restoration work and who has a reputation

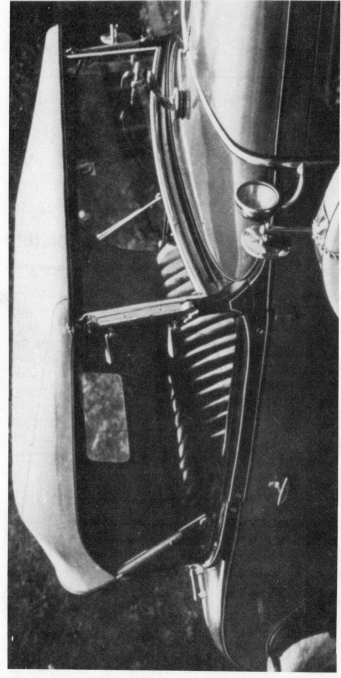

Fig. 14-1. The top and upholstery of this 1931 Model A Ford were made from readily available upholstery kits! Owner: Ernest Swanson, Ridgefield, CT.

Fig. 14-2. An upholstery kit was used in restoring the seats of this Model A Ford rumble seat. Owner: Ernest Swanson, Ridgefield, CT.

Fig. 14-3. Cloth upholstery being professionally installed on a Model A Ford Sedan (courtesy of Hibernia Auto Restorations Inc., Hibernia, NJ).

for quality work among the members of your club. This type of work is expensive and if you are willing to entrust your work to a less experienced upholsterer you may save a bit. See "Automotive Seat Covers, Tops & Upholstery" in your telephone book Yellow Pages.

An upholsterer with no experience in restoration work will have to be "educated." He must understand that the construction of the upholstery must be *exactly* like the original. Let him know that "short cuts" will not be acceptable. Then tell him that you will not hold him to a fixed estimate in advance, that you will pay him fairly based on the time he spends on the job. Most likely this type of upholsterer will not have the correct materials as used on your car. You will have to buy the correct materials after he tells you the number of yards he will require for each part.

Again, reconsider the more expensive professional restoration upholsterer. He may be more satisfactory in the long run. He will have the correct materials or will get them. He will guarantee a perfect professional job. You will not have to supervise him each step of the way.

For a detailed look at upholstery work, see also *Car Interior Restoration*, TAB book #2102.

Chapter 15
Preparing For Show

The most important event in the hobby of car collecting is the vast Hershey Show, held in October of each year at Hershey, Pennsylvania by the Antique Automobile Club of America. It is the largest show held in America and most experts consider it the best run, boasting the most objective standards of judging in the hobby. The A.A.C.A. judging procedure leaves little or no room for a judge to be influenced by his own personal likes and dislikes. The procedure in other clubs is not always as fair and personal favoritism of a particular judge can sometimes ruin an otherwise delightful meet. Discuss this subject with the more experienced members of your club. In most clubs this is not a problem but even when it is a problem it can usually be solved by joint action by the members.

Learn the Rules

To compete successfully you must *know the rules!* Ask your club for a copy of their "Judging Form" and "Official Judging Manual." A thorough understanding of these documents will give you the best chance to take a First Prize.

The "perfect" car is one that is in precisely the same condition as it was when it left the factory as a new car. Therefore judging for show is based on the authenticity, workmanship, and maintenance of each component. Although the car must be driven on to the show grounds, no further detailed check of its mechanical condition will be made. A copy of the A.A.C.A. Judging Form (Table 15-1) is reproduced here and the following is part of the instructions to the judges about the use of this form (under the A.A.C.A. system a perfect score is 400):

Authenticity, Workmanship, Maintenance Considered

"The correct procedure for use of this form is to first inspect the vehicle. When a fault is found, look for the component under consideration on the form and enter the number of points to be deducted in the appropriate block. Judge each component for authenticity, workmanship and maintenance. Deduct the maximum points indicated for non-authentic or missing components. Do not deduct more than the maximum points indicated for any single listed item. When there is multiple use of a component such as doors, lights and wheels, the indicated deduction may be taken for each individual part (Example: If a vehicle has four non-authentic wheels, the deduction is four times the three point maximum deduction for a single wheel, or twelve points total). When judging condition of finish of any component, deduct points for faults such as alignment of components, depth of finish, runs, orange peel, rust, dents, scratches, cracks, lack of paint, lack of plating, etc. Plating must be of the authentic type for the vehicle being judged. Chrome plating prior to 1928 is improper unless authenticity can be documented by the owner (Hard Nickel is not considered a deductible feature). Deduct one point for each component with non-authentic plating, with a maximum deduction of ten points per vehicle for non-authentic plating. Do not deduct points for slight defects which may have been caused en route to the meet. For example, minor scratches, dents, grease, oil and dirt which obviously are new."

Over Restoration

In their Judging Manual the A.A.C.A. takes up the subject of "over restoration":

"Recently there has been much comment, some unfavorable, on the subject of over restoration. From a subjective standpoint this may be commendable. But it greatly complicates the problem of judging. The over restored car should not be given any preference over other cars and

Table 15-1. A Typical A.A.C.A. Judging Form

MEET: _____ ENTRY No: _____ OWNER: _____ MAKE: _____ YEAR: _____ CLASS: _____

EXTERIOR

EXTERIOR	MAX	DED
Body Door	5	
Fender	5	
Hood	5	
Panel	5	
Trim/Striping	3	
Light Head	5	
Side	3	
Tail	3	
Driving	3	
Radiator Shell	5	
Grill		
Ornament		
Top (Hard)	3	
Horn	3	
Mirror	3	
Windshield Frame	3	
Wind. Wiper	3	
Door Handle	2	
Running Board	5	
Splash Apron	3	
Gas Gen./Tank	3	
Beading/Welting	(20)	
Incorrect Body	(15)	
Material		
Color	(10)	
Other:		
TOTAL DEDUCTION		

INTERIOR

INTERIOR	MAX	DED
Top (Soft):	5	
Missing (Irised)	(20)	
Down	(10)	
Material	5	
Trim	3	
Fastener	1*	
Top Iron/Bow	3	
Side Curtain	3	2
(Missing)	(10)	
Headliner	5	
Seat Cushion/Back	5	
Side Panel	3	
Door Panel	5	
Window Frame	3	
Door Sill	3	
Floor Cover (Mat)	3	
Steering Wheel	3	
Pedal/Lever	2	
Dashboard	3	
Instrument	5	
Foot Rest	3	
Tonneau Wind.	5	
Glass	3	
Trim	3	
Incr. Uphol. Mat'l.	(10)	
Other:		
TOT'L DEDUCTION		

CHASSIS

CHASSIS	MAX	DED
Axle Front	5	
Rear	(20)	
Trans. Drive Line	(10)	
Snubber/Shock	3	
Gas Tank	3	
Steering Assembly	5	
Pow. Steering (Add)	(10)	
Brake	3	
Body Bolt	1*	
Lube Fitting	1*	
Lack of Lube	1	
Excess Lube	1	
Exhaust System	5	
Tire	3	
Wheel	3	
Rim	5	
Lock Ring	3	
Hub Cap	2	
Valve Stem	1	
Cover	3	
Spring	3	
Spring Cover	2	
Frame	5	
Bumper	3	
Overdrive (Add)	(10)	
Tire Carrier/Cover		
Other:		
TOTAL DEDUCTION		

ENGINE

ENGINE	MAX	DED
Block	5	
Head	5	
Crankcase	5	
Manifold	3	
Radiator Core	10	
Starter	5	
Starter (Add)	(10)	
Generator	5	
Fuel Supply	5	
Fuel Supply (Add)	(10)	
Carburetor	5	
Magneto/Dist.	3	
Coil/Horn	3	
Clamp	1*	
Belt	2	
Firewall	3	
Priming Cup	1	
Waterpump	5	
Terminal	1*	
Splash Pan	3	
Wiring	3	
Taps/Tubing	1	
Filter/Fan	3	
Incorrect Engine	(20)	
Ov'hd Valves (Add)	(10)	
Gauge/Control	3	
Other:		
TOTAL DEDUCTION		

SUMMARY

AWARD
Junior 1st
2nd
3rd
Multiple Award

DEDUCTIONS
Exterior - _____
Interior - _____
Chassis - _____
Engine - _____
TOTAL - _____

SCORE

Perfect Score	400
Total Deductions	
NET SCORE	

REQUIRED MINIMUM POINTS
1st - 365, 2nd - 330, 3rd - 295
(Multiple awards for scores within 10 points of highest scoring car in each award).

APPROVED
TEAM CAPTAIN _____
DEPUTY JUDGE _____
DEPUTY JUDGE _____

NOTES: (Add) Non-authentic accessory added   (10) Mandatory deduction   * Max. deduction 10 points per vehicle should be scored according to its appearance as it left the factory."

Find out how your own club feels about over restoration before you go too far with your own restoration.

Once your car is restored, preparing for show is simply a meticulous clean up job covering every part of the car. If you use your car quite often the job will take much longer than if you keep the car exclusively for show occasions. The ultimate in this approach are those who keep their car in a heated garage wrapped in a custom made car cover and bring it to a meet in an enclosed trailer! Preparation for these people is usually limited to a thorough dusting of the car and repolishing of the bright work.

Pre-Show Cleaning

For most of us preparation for a show means hard work for several days with a vast array of waxes, polishes, preservatives, stain removers, grease cutters and solvents. Most of these are available from any well stocked hardware or automotive supply store. A few products are worth special mention. One is "Armor All," a liquid which preserves rubber and alleges to prevent the fine cracking usually found on old tires or anything else made of rubber. It also cleans the rubber and gives it that "as new" look. (Armor All is made by Very Important Products, Newport Beach, CA 92660.) Another good one is "Lexol" which softens and preserves leather and is available in most hardware stores.

Chapter 16
Storing The Car

First of all you must accept the fact that extended storage is destructive. In the normal course of time, even in a heated garage, engines will seize, metals will rust and corrode, paint will oxidize, gaskets will dry out, gasoline and oil will turn to gum, and within two or three years the car may require a complete rebuild!

Slowing the Deterioration

By the following specific procedures, the process of destruction can be greatly slowed or completely stopped, but only on a year to year basis. There is no method of preservation which will preserve a car indefinitely.

Certain precautions must be taken regardless of the number of months or years you intend to leave the car in storage. The following rules are basic precautions to be observed:

● Store the car in a dry garage. If you live in a cold climate the garage should be heated.

● Change the oil and refill with a light-weight oil such as 20-weight.

● Remove the spark plugs, fill with oil and replace the spark plugs.

● Drain the cooling system and refill with antifreeze and rust inhibitor. For cars that have well-worn engines, use an alcohol base anti-freeze. The permanent type antifreezes tend to find minute holes which can create leaks.

● Cover the air inlet on the carburetors and the end of the exhaust pipe. This is easily done with doubled over plastic sheet and electric tape.

● Remove the battery and store it in a warm place. Do not store a battery on a concrete floor.

● Thoroughly wax all painted and plated surfaces.

● Buy four jack stands to place under either side of the rear axle and the front frame members to hold the car off the ground.

● Keep a dust cover over the car and leave it loose to allow air to circulate underneath.

● Keep the clutch pedal depressed by wedging a 2″ x 4″ piece of wood the right length wedged between the clutch pedal and the bottom of the driver's seat, or wedge the clutch pedal open from the engine side of the firewall. In either case this will prevent the clutch plate from adhering to the flywheel due to a build-up of humidity.

SHORT-TERM STORAGE

For short-term storage, less than one year, leave the car "wet," i.e., the cooling system full of water and antifreeze, the engine full of oil, and the gas tank full. This will prevent the drying out of gaskets and seals. However, to keep the carburetor from gumming up you must run the engine at least once a month for about thirty minutes to bring the engine up to full operating temperature.

If you will not be able to start the car once a month you should prepare it with very little gas left in the tank, run it until all of the gas is used up (this will clear the carburetors of gas) and *then* fill the gas tank full. This will prevent the formation of corrosion in the gas tank.

PREPARING AFTER STORAGE

Starting a car after a long period of storage involves a series of prudent precautions and a certain element of luck. I have seen cars started after many years of storage with only a fresh battery, a set of jumper cables and a small can of gasoline.

If you have the facilities available it is prudent to follow a few simple rules to avoid damaging the engine:

● Establish that the engine is "free," i.e., that the crankshaft, rods, and pistons are free to move. This can be checked by removing the spark plugs and turning the engine by means of a crank or by placing the transmission in 1st gear or Reverse and rocking the car back and forth. If the engine is not "free" add penetrating oil through the spark plug holes and try again. If this doesn't work the engine should be taken apart and rebuilt.

● Drain the oil and look for pieces of babbit. If you find any don't start the engine. Again, an engine rebuild is indicated. Otherwise, refill with fresh oil.

● Drain the gas tank. Flush and refill with fresh gas.

● Charge the battery or, better yet, install a new fully-charged battery.

● Open the distributor and check the points. If they are pitted, file them even.

● Clean the spark plugs or replace them with new spark plugs.

● You are now ready to start the engine. First, engage the starter to turn over the engine with the ignition off. Watch the oil pressure gauge and keep the engine turning until oil pressure is indicated. Now, prime the carburetors with a few tablespoons of gas and try to start the engine with the ignition on. Be sure the choke control is operating freely. If you flood the carburetors, press the accelerator pedal all the way to the floor and try again.

● If the engine will not start check to be sure that gas is reaching the carburetors. If not, you may have to rebuild the fuel pump. Also, check that electric current is reaching the spark plugs by holding a plug lead very close to the spark plug. If there is no spark, check the ground wire and the hot wire to the coil to be sure all connections are tight. You may require a new coil and/or condenser but at this point you should get an experienced mechanic to assist you.

● If the engine does start, let it run for at least 30 minutes before attempting to drive it. This will allow the engine to thoroughly warm up and every part will be lubricated.

Postscript

Those of us who have spent many years in restoration work understand only too well that "Murphy's Law" is usually in full operation. "Murphy's Law" is simply that "If anything can go wrong, it will."

Ken Painter of the Maserati Club has stated the case very well and I can do no better than to quote him:

"I list below some of the grim facts about restoration work that I have learned the hard way over the years. These gems contain no mechanical secrets, no short cuts to success; on the contrary, they go a long way towards explaining why you will never succeed in completing your restoration as quickly or as economically as you had expected:

Rule 1. If anything can go wrong, it will.

Rule 2. Interchangeable parts won't.

Rule 3. Any wire or tube cut to length will be too short.

Rule 4. Availability of a part is inversely proportional to your need for it.

Rule 5. Tolerances will accumulate unidirectionally towards maximum difficulty of assembly.

Rule 6. After a part has been fully assembled, extra components will be found on the bench.

Rule 7. A dropped tool will land where it can do most damage, or where it will be most inaccessible. Sometimes it will do both. (This is known as the law of selective gravitation.)

Rule 8. Components that must not and cannot be assembled incorrectly, will be.

Rule 9. Any error that can creep in, will. It will be in the direction that will do most damage.

Rule 10. All constants are variable.

Rule 11. The most logical way to assemble a part will be the wrong way.

Rule 12. Dimensions will always be expressed in the least usable terms.

Rule 13. If a part can be installed incorrectly, that is what you will do.

Rule 14. An adjustable spanner used to remove a component will either be too tight or too slack to replace the same part, even if you try to replace it immediately.

Rule 15. Hermetic seals will leak.

Rule 16. After the last 16 screws are removed from a component, you will find that you are dismantling the wrong part.

Rule 17. To estimate the time a restoration will take, carefully work out how long you expect the job to take, then treble it. To estimate the cost, carefully work out all known expenditure, then quadruple it. You will still be wrong, but not as wrong as you would have been if you had believed your first estimates.

Of course, you won't always find that the first 16 of these rules will apply at the same time, Rule 17 operates constantly though. Even so, it can be postulated as Rule 18 that a random percentage will constantly be operating to your disadvantage.

If you still feel that the restoration game is worth a try, then all I can suggest is a visit to your doctor. He will be able to arrange a suitable specialist appointment for you. Whatever you do, don't come to me for help. You see, I've just bought a lovely 3500 GT, but it has a broken gearbox . . ."

Appendix A
Restoration Shops in the
United States and Canada

Alabama

Automobile Restoration Co.
Rte. 5, Box 856
Wetumpka, AL 36092
205-567-8974

Manager: Jerry Boothe. Specializes in complete restorations on antique and classic autos

Lonsdale Restorations
441 Clay St.
Montgomery, AL 36104

Specializes in antiques and classics

Arizona

Franklin Service Co.
1405 E. Kleindale Road
Tucson, AZ 85719
602-326-8038

Owner: Thomas H. Hubbard. Specializes in classic era Franklins. Restores for Harrah

California

Andrews Auto Restoration Center
4921 Folsom Blvd.
Sacramento, CA 95819
916-452-8127

Owner: Phil H. Andrews. Specializes in complete restoration of classic and special interest cars

Bill's Antique Body Works
908 9th St.
Turlock, CA 95380
209-634-7996

Owner: W.A. Borba. Specializes in body building and complete restorations

Custom Auto Service
302 French St.
Santa Ana, CA 92701
714-543-2980

Specializes in classic and postwar Packards Various hourly rates

Griswold Co.
1809 San Pablo Ave.
Berkeley, CA 94702
415-527-5818

Owner: Stephen W. Griswold Complete restorations Aluminum bodies

William H. Lauver
140 South "B" St.
Tustin, CA 92680

L & M Auto
11562 Santa Monica Blvd.
Los Angeles, CA 90025

Nethercutt Laboratories
15180 Bledsoe St.
Sylmar, CA 91342

Owner: Jack B. Nethercutt

Mr. O. A. "Bunny" Phillips
8724 E. Garvey Ave.
Rosemead, CA 91770
213-280-3168

Specializes in complete restoration of Bugattis. Since 1930

Gene Sherman
501 W. Maple Ave.
Orange, CA 92666

Colorado

Antique Auto House, Inc.
3329 N. Garfield - P.O. Box 685
Loveland, CO 80537
303-667-7040

Owner: John R. & Nancy J. Bergquist. Specialize in buying and selling antique and classic cars and fire trucks

Connecticut

Automotive Restorations Inc.
50 Embree St.
Stratford, CT 06497
203-377-6745

Hoe Sportcar
446 Newtown Turnpike
Weston, CT 06883
203-227-6462

Owner: Jim Hoe. Specializes in mechanical restoration of Duesenbergs and other antiques and classics.

Reuter's Coachworks, Inc.
27R Catoonah St.
Ridgefield, CT 06877
203-438-6417

Owner: Gus Reuter. No mechanical work. Specializes in restoration of great antique and classic cars

Vintage Auto Restorations, Inc.
Box 83, 27R Catoonah St.
Ridgefield, CT 06877
203-438-4946

Owner: Don Lefferts. Specializes in complete restorations of vintage and classic cars. Bugatti specialist. Vintage sportcar overhaul and repair

Florida

Antique Autos of America
611 Commerce Dr.
Largo, FL 33540
813-586-2822

Auto Rebuilding and Restoration Services Inc.
P.O. Box 96
Florahome, FL 32635
904-659-2163

Belote's Bayshore Garage
949 Broadway
Dunedin, FL 33528
813-733-7350

Owner: Philip W. Belote. Specializes in Marmon 8's. Mechanical restorations also

Horseless Carriage Shop
1881 Main St. (Hwy. 580)
Dunedin, FL 33528
813-733-9340

Manager: Edward "Bud" Josey

Illinois

The Antique Auto House
205 E. Kehoe
Carol Stream, IL 60187

Specializes in Rolls-Royce

Indiana

Custom Trim
1332 W. Main
Ft. Wayne, IN 46808
219-422-1633

Custom automotive interiors; classics, antiques, customs

S.R.M. Classic Cars Inc.
1633 W. Lusher Ave.
Elkhart, IN 46514
219-293-1454

Complete or partial restorations

Kansas

Sunflower Restoration Center
P. O. Box 502 - 15480 Henry Ford Rd.
Olathe, KS 66061

Complete or partial restorations

Kentucky

The Antique Auto Shop
603 Lytle Ave.
Elsmere, KY 41018
606-342-8363

Partial or complete restorations on vintage and antique cars

Pearson & Marzian, Inc.
501 E. St. Catherine St.
Louisville, KY 40203
502-585-2475

Owner: Kenneth Mitsch. Complete antique and classic upholstery restoration

Massachusetts

Dearborn Automobile Co.
16 Maple St. at Rte. 1
Topsfield, MA 01983
617-887-6544

Mercedes-Benz

Moineau Car Co.
419A Lincoln St.
Marlboro, MA 01752
617-481-6585

Complete restoration work

River Street Motors
106 River St.
Dedham, MA 02026
617-329-2480

Restoration of antique, classic and special interest autos, semi- or complete

Vetco New England Inc.
P.O. Box 123
Northfield, MA 01360
413-498-2626

Manager:
Wes Ives. Complete res-
toration of antique
and classic cars

Michigan

Auto Restorations Inc.
441 Elmwood
Troy, MI 48084

Clark-Patton Inc.
4775 Curtis
Plymouth, MI 48170
313-662-9033

Manager: T. Terry
Patton. Restoration of
antique and
classic cars

Leonard A. Davis
1345 Whitney Dr.
Watkins Lake
Pontiac, MI 48054

Specializes in brass
era antiques

Fleet Supply Corp.
2896 Central Ave.
Detroit, MI 48209
313-843-2200

Owner: Thomas
Deptulski. Complete
restoration, machine shop,
Model T & A parts. Spe-
cializes in brass era cars

Andy Hotton Assoc.
510 Savage Rd.
Belleville, MI 48111
313-697-7129

Manager: Donald J.
Hotton. Specializes in
Ford products only;
includes Lincolns

Jerry Kiefer
33711 Edmonton
Farmingham, MI 48204

Specializes in classic cars

Ted Ongena
2145 S. Lapeer Rd.
Lapeer, MI 48446

Specializes in antiques

Minnesota

Johnson Iron & Machine Co.
P.O. Box 435
1201 De Mers Ave.
East Grand Forks, MN 56721
218-773-0525

Owner:
Melvin Johnson
Specializes in antiques

Sig Monson A.B.
4731 Grand Ave.
Duluth, MN 55807
218-624-0950

*Specializes in body
restoration and painting*

Missouri

Memoryville, U.S.A.
Jct. Hwy I-44 and 63 North
Rolla, MO
314-364-1810

*Manager:
George L.
Carney. Specializes in complete antique
car restorations*

Jake's - Farrington Machine Service
Rt. 4
Lebanon, MO 65536

Nevada

Adams Custom Engines Inc.
806 Glendale Ave.
Sparks, NV 89431
702-358-8070

*Owner:
Everett J. Adams.
Complete restoration
facilities*

James Gullihur
P.O. Box 345
Fernley, NV 89408

*Complete restoration of
antique, classic and
special interest cars*

New Jersey

Antique Auto, Inc.
Northfield, NJ 08225

Antique Auto Shop, Inc.
R.D. #2
Box 281A
Pleasantville, NJ 08232
609-927-8729

*Owner: Ralph T.
Buckley. Specializes in complete
restoration of Simplex Mercer
and other antique
and classic cars*

James A. Cular
Antique Auto Restoration
R.D. 1, Box 825, Rte. 15
Lafayette, NJ 07848
201-383-8811

Robert J. Gassaway, Inc.
519 Main St.
South Amboy, NJ 08879
201-721-2260

Henry's Antique Car Shop
P. O. Box 133 - 804 E.
Somers Landing Road
Oceanville, NJ 08231
609-652-1373

Owner:
Henry Heinsohn.
Specializes in full or
partial restoration
of all makes

Hibernia Auto Restorations, Inc.
Maple Terrace
Hibernia, NJ 07842
201-627-1882

Manager:
Jim Cox. Complete
machine and electrical
shop, Nitrocellulose lacquer
manufactured, engine and
chassis rebuilding body,
woodwork, plating, graining,
welding, sandblasting and
steamcleaning; on all cars

Hullco-Layton Garage
Box 78
Layton, NJ 07851
201-948-4380

Antique auto resto-
rations; metal repair, fabrica-
tion, painting,
pin striping

The Restoration Shop
R.D. 1, Box 228
Jamesburg, NJ 08831
201-521-1128

Owner: Earl Lewis.
Complete and partial
restorations;
engine rebuilding

Schaeffer & Long Inc.
210 Davis Rd.
Magnolia, NJ 08049
609-784-4044

Manager:
Fred Hock. Complete
and partial antique
and classic auto
restoration

Vintage Auto Restorations
101 Atlantic Ave.
Spring Lake, NJ 07762
201-449-8525

Complete and
partial restorations

New York

Coachwork Unlimited
370-D Commack Rd.
Deer Park, NY 11729
516-667-2679

Complete restoration
services; including
woodwork, mechanical
and engine rebuilding

90

Grand Prix SSR Co.
36 Route 25A
E. Setauket, NY 11733
516-751-8700

Specializes in restoring Ferrari and other sports/racing cars. Aluminum coachwork

Heritage Automotive Restorations
36 River Road
Pawling, NY 12564
914-855-5388

Ohio

Paul Beechy
Winesburg, OH 44690

Budley & Sons
5599 Highland Rd.
Cleveland, OH 44143

**Cobb's Antique
Auto Restoration Inc.**
717 Western Ave.
Washington Court House, OH 43160
614-335-7489

Owner: Eddie Cobb. Complete restoration and woodworking on all prewar cars

**Feicht's Antique &
Classic Auto Restoration**
21 W. Park Ave.
Columbiana, OH 44408
216-482-9221

Owner: Bruce and Carolyn Feicht. Complete restoration all makes and models; wood, radiators, mechanical, body and painting

Vintage Auto Shop
430 Mill St.
Cincinnati, OH 45215
513-821-2159

Owner: Ned Herrmann. Specializes in Rolls-Royces

Oklahoma

Classic Motors, Inc.
1046 N.W. 71st ST.
Oklahoma City, OK 73116
405-848-2456

Val H. Curry
1531 N.E. 50th
Oklahoma City, OK 73111
405-424-5434

Mail order only.
"Home individual
restorations"

Pennsylvania

Durland's Antique
Auto Restoration Center
34 Church ST.
Swoyerville, PA 18704
717-287-5559

Owner: Durland Edwards.
Twenty years of antique
and classic car
restoration. Over
forty national first
prize winners

Glazier's Mustang Barn Inc.
531 Wambold Rd.
Souderton, PA 18964
215-723-9674

Owner: Fred
Glazier, Jr. Parts
and restorations
specializing in
1964 1/2 -1968 Mustangs

Richard's Auto Restoration
R.D. #3, Box 83
Wyoming, PA 18644
717-333-4191

Owner: Richard Zim

Stanley Sales and Service
C.S. Amsley, R.D. 2
Box 69
St. Thomas, PA 17252

Complete steam
car restoration

Wilkinson & Sharp
233 Philmont Ave.
Feasterville, PA 19047
215-357-8090

Managers: Stan Wilkinson
& Arthur Sharp.
Complete antique and
classic car restoration.
Have restored cars for
some of the best known
collectors in U.S.

Rhode Island

Bassett's Restoration
& Supplies
P.O. Box 145
Peace Dale, R.I. 02883
401-789-9378

Owner: Bill &
Marion Bassett. Parts,
interiors and
restoration for
Jaguars

Texas

Coleman & Oquin Restoration
1569 Sheffield
Houston, TX 77015
713-455-2355

Complete restoration of antique and vintage cars

Antique Car Barn
4282 Hwy. 90 E.
San Antonio, TX 78219
512-333-2541

Complete restorations, specializing in chassis

Jack Hildreth
7305 Lakehurst
Dallas, TX 75203
214-369-2748

Parthenon Motors Ltd.
204 Dinn Rd.
San Antonio, TX 78218

Bugatti, Bucialli, Rover

Virginia

White Post Restorations
White Post, VA 22663
703-837-1140

Frame-up restorations

Wisconsin

Dick's Autobody
Marshfield, WI 54449

Auto Strippers and Restorers, Inc.
900 W. Commerce St.
Cambria, WI 53923
414-348-5868

Auto stripping and restoration

Ron-Lee Automotive Restoration
1402 Wisconsin Ave.
Grafton, WI 53024
414-375-1390

Complete restorations

Canada

Fawcett Motor Carriage Co. Ltd.
106 Palmerston Ave.
Whitby, Ontario
416-668-4446

Owner: Ron Fawcett

John E. Brown Motors Ltd.
Gorrie, Ontario NOGIO
519-335-3325

Owner:
John Brown.
Complete restorations;
custom-built trailers

W. J. Oatman
75 Bartley Dr.
Toronto 16, Ontario
Rose Saunders
Watford, Ontario.

Appendix B
Antique, Classic
and Historic Car Clubs

General Clubs

Antique Automobile Club of America
501 W. Governor Road
Hershey, PA 17033

Classic Car Club of America*
P.O. Box 443
Madison, NJ 07940

Contemporary Historical Vehicle Association
P.O. Box 40
Antioch, TN 37013

Custom Coach Builders of America
Box 100
Wittman, MD 21676

Horseless Carriage Club of America
9031 E. Florence Ave.
Downey, CA 90240

The Milestone Car Society*
P.O. Box 50850
Indianapolis, IN 46250

The Society of Automotive Historians
Charles L. Betts, Jr.
2105 Stackhouse Dr.
Yardley, PA 19067

Steam Automobile Club of America Inc.
1937 E. 71st St.
Chicago, IL 60649

Veteran Motor Car Club of America
c/o Dr. Robt. H. DeHart
105 Elm St.
Andover, MA 01810

The Vintage Sports Car Club
2035 Greenwood
Wilmette, IL 60091

Vintage Sports Car Club of America
A. S. Carroll, Secretary
170 Wetherill Road
Garden City, NY 11570

*Lists of eligible cars will be found at end of this section.

AC

AC Owners Club, American Centre
Daniel G. Everett
Vinemont Road No. 6
Sinking Springs, PA 19608

Alfa Romeo

Alfa Romeo Owners Club
Box 331
Northbrook, IL 60062

Alvis

Alvis Owners Club
308 Dogwood Lane
Wallingford, PA 19086
Alvis Owners Club
The Hill House
Rushock, Nr. Droitwich,
Worcs., England

American Austin/Bantam

American Austin/Bantam
P. O. Box 328
Morris, NY 13808
Pacific Bantam Austin Club
4636 Midsite Ave.
Covina, CA 81722

Amilcar

Amilcar Register
West Hays,
Rockbourne, Fordingbridge,
Hants., SP6 3NL, England

Arnolt-Bristol

Arnolt-Bristol Registry
Robert Schifrin
9382 Gina Drive
West Chester, OH 45069

Aston-Martin

Aston Martin Owners Club Ltd.
Charles L. Turner
195 Mt. Paran Road, N.W.
Atlanta, GA 30327

Auburn

Auburn-Cord-Duesenberg Club Inc.
Box 11635
Palo Alto, CA 94306

Bentley

The Bentley Drivers Club
Andrew T. Fisher
317 Greenbank Ave.
Duarte, CA 91010

Bugatti

The American Bugatti Club
8724 E. Garvey Ave.
Rosemead, CA 91770
Bugatti Owners Club
Sir Anthony Stamer, Secretary
Cedar Court, 9 The Fair Mile
Henley-on-Thames, Oxfordshire,
RG9 2JT, England

Buick

Buick Club of America
P.O. Box 898
Garden Grove, CA 92642
Buick Collectors Club of America
Sidney Aberman
4730 Centre Ave.
Pittsburgh, PA 15213

Cadillac

Cadillac Automobile Club
P.O. Box 2842
Pasadena, CA 91105
Cadillac La Salle Club
3340 Poplar Drive
Warren, MI 48091

Chevrolet

The Vintage Chevrolet Club of America, Inc.
P.O. Box 5387
Orange, CA 92667
Vintage Chevrolet Club
1 Beechwood Avenue
Crescent Trailer Park
Gloucester, NJ 08030
National Corvette Owners Association
404 S. Maple Ave.
Falls Church, VA 22046
National Corvette Restorers Society
P.O. Box 81663
Lincoln, NB 68501
Vintage Corvette Club of America
c/o Ed Thiebaud
2359 W. Adams
Fresno, CA 93706

Chrysler

Chrysler 300 Club
Bill Purcell
629 Berkley Ave.
Elmhurst, IL 60126
Airflow Club of America Inc.
RD 1
Arkport, NY 14807

The Imperial Owners Club
P.O. Box 991
Scranton, PA 18503
Plymouth 4 & 6 Cylinder Owners Club Inc.
203 Main St.
E. Cavalier, ND 58220
The W.P.C. Club (Walter P. Chrysler)
(Plymouth, Dodge, DeSoto, Chrysler Imperial and related cars)
P.O. Box 4705
N. Hollywood, CA 91603
Dodge, Chrysler, Plymouth, DeSoto Maxwell Club
982 E. 81st St.
Brooklyn, NY 11236

Cord

Auburn-Cord-Duesenberg Club Inc.
Box 11635
Palo Alto, CA 94306

Corvair

Corvair Society of America
P.O. Box 2488
Pensacola, FL 32503

Crosley

Crosley Automobile Club
c/o Jim Bollman
4825 Ridge Rd. E.
Williamson, NY 14589

Daimler

Daimler Club
c/o Gifford Dart
1500 Story Rd.
San Jose, CA 95122

The Daimler & Lanchester Owners Club of North America
78 Williams St.
Streetsville, Ontario, Canada
L5M 1J3

DB

DB & Panhard Registry
See "Panhard"

Delage

Les Amis de Delage
4 Boulevard Garbriel
Guist'hau
44000-NANTES, France

DeSoto

DeSoto Club of America
c/o Walter O'Kelly
105 E. 96th St.
Kansas City, MO 64114

Dodge

Dodge, Chrysler, Plymouth, DeSoto, Maxwell Club
982 E. 81st St.
Brooklyn, NY 11236

Duesenberg

Auburn-Cord-Duesenberg Club, Inc.
Box 11635
Palo Alto, CA 94306

Essex

Hudson-Essex-Terraplane Club
100 E. Cross St.
Ypsilanti, MI 48197

Facel

Facel Club
Richard A. Neary
528 Rahway Ave.
Woodbridge, NJ 07095

Ferrari

Ferrari Club of America
Dyke Ridgley
1474 Greendell Drive
Decatur, IL 62526

Ferrari Owners Club (G.B.)
Sir Anthony Stamer, Secretary
Cedar Court, 9 The Fair Mile
Henley-on-Thames, Oxfordshire RG9 2JT,
England

Ferrari Owners Club (U.S.)
Ed Niles, Membership Chairman
3460 Wiltshire Blvd. Suite 1010
Los Angeles, CA 90010

Fiat

Fiat Club of America Inc.
Box 192
Somerville, MA 02143

Ford

Model A Restorers Club Inc.
Box 1930 A
Somerville, MA 02143

Model A Ford Club of America
Box 1791
Whittier, CA 90603

Model T Ford Club International
P.O. Box 915
Elgin, IL 60120

The Model T Ford Club of America
Box 7400
Burbank, CA 91510

Early Ford V8 Club of America
P.O. Box 2122
San Leandro, CA 94577

Fabulous Fifties Ford Club
729 Dellcrest Way
Escondido, CA 92027

Ford Mercury Club of America Inc.
P.O. Box 3551
Hayward, CA 94540

Franklin

The H. H. Franklin Club
Cazenovia College
Cazenovia, NY 13035

Frazer

Kaiser-Frazer Owners Club International
c/o W. C. Ashton
4130 New River Stage
New River, AZ 85029

Kaiser-Frazer Owners Club of America, Inc.
c/o Jesse E. Ehlers
4015 S. Forest
Independence, MO 64052

Frazer-Nash

Frazer Nash Section of VSCC
20 School Hill
Walton 1e Wolds
Loughborough, Leics., England

G. M. Cars

General Motors Restorers Club
P.O. Box 307, Highland Station
Springfield, MA 01109

Graham

Graham Owner's Club International
P.O. Box 105
Burlington, MA 01803

Graham & Graham-Paige Registry
Andrew Wittenborn
30 N. Broadway, Apt. 5E
White Plains, NY 10601

Hispano-Suiza

Hispano-Suiza Society
230 Park Ave.
Suite 1624
New York, NY 10017

Hudson

Hudson-Essex-Terraplane Club
100 E. Cross St.
Ypsilanti, MI 48197

Hupmobile

Hupmobile Club Inc.
Box AA
Rosemead, CA 91770

Isotta-Fraschini

Isotta-Fraschini Owners Association
9704 Illinois St.
Hebron, IL 60034

Jaguar

Classic Jaguar Association Inc.
c/o Richard Zolla
1138 Dorset Lane
Costa Mesa, CA 92626
Jaguar Clubs of North America Inc.
c/o F. S. Horner
P.O. Box 423
Locust Valley, NY 11560
EJAG North America
1 Acton Road
Westford, MA 01886

Kaiser

Kaiser-Frazer Owners Club International
c/o W. C. Ashton
4130 New River Stage
New River, AZ 85029
Kaiser-Frazer Owners Club of America, Inc.
c/o Jesse E. Ehlers
4015 S. Forest
Independence, MO 64052

Knight

The Willys-Overland-Knight Registry
241 Orchard Drive
Dayton, OH 45419

Lagonda

The Lagonda Club
c/o R. T. Crane
10 Crestwood Trail
Lake Mohawk
Sparta, NJ 07871

Lancia

Lancia Motor Club
"New Grass," Down Ampney,
Cirencester,
Gloucestershire, GL7 5QW,
England

La Salle

Cadillac La Salle Club
3340 Poplar Drive
Warren, MI 48091

Lincoln

Lincoln Continental Owners Club
P.O. Box 549
Nogales, AZ 85621
Lincoln Zephyr Owners Club
P.O. Box 185
Middletown, PA 17057

Marmon

Marmon Owners Club
629 Orangewood Drive
Dundin, FL 33528

Maxwell

Dodge, Chrysler, Plymouth, DeSoto, Maxwell Club
982 E. 81st St.
Brooklyn, NY 11236

Mercedes-Benz

Mercedes-Benz Club of America Inc.
7502 E. Lincoln Drive
Scottsdale, AZ 85253

Mercury

Ford Mercury Club of America
P.O. Box 3551
Hayward, CA 94540

Messerschmitt

Messerschmitt Owners Club
c/o Les Klinge
39 Sylvan Way
West Caldwell, NJ 07006

M.G.

M. G. Car Club "Triple M" Register (Pre-War Only)
11 Orchard End Ave.
Amersham, Bucks., England
New England MG "T" Register Ltd.
Drawer #220
Oneonta, NY 13820
The M.G. Car Club Ltd.
c/o F. S. Horner
P.O. Box 423
Locust Valley, NY 11560

Nash

Nash-Healey Car Club International
c/o Ray Soles
R.D.1, Lakeshore Drive, Box A161
Addison, PA 15411
Nash Car Club of America
R #1, Box 253, Elvira Rd.
Clinton, IA 52732

Oldsmobile

Oldsmobile Club of America
145 Latona Road
Rochester, NY 14626

Overland

The Willys-Overland-Knight Registry
241 Orchard Drive
Dayton, OH 45419

Packard

Packard Automobile Classics
P.O. Box 2808
Oakland, CA 94618
Packards International Motor Car Club
302 French St.
Santa Ana, CA 92701

Panhard

DB & Panhard Registry
c/o H. G. Schneider
Blair Academy
Blairstown, NJ 07825

Pierce-Arrow

Pierce-Arrow Society, Inc.
135 Edgerton St.
Rochester, NY 14607

Plymouth

Dodge, Chrysler, Plymouth, DeSoto, Maxwell Club
982 E. 81st St.
Brooklyn, NY 11236

Plymouth Owners Club
c/o R. E. Bender
RD #1, Box 306
Jeannette, PA 15644

Pontiac

Pontiac-Oakland Club International
P.O. Box 5108
Salem, OR 97304

Porsche

Porsche Club of America
5616 Clermont Drive
Alexandria, VA 22310
Porsche Owners Club
P.O. Box 54910, Terminal Annex
Los Angeles, CA 90054

Railton

The Railton Owners Club
c/o Barrie McKenzie
Fairmiles
Barnes Hall Rd., Burncross,
Sheffield, S30 4RF, England

Riley

The Riley Motor Club USA Inc.
P.O. Box 4162
Anaheim, CA 92803

Rolls-Royce

Rolls-Royce Owners Club Inc.
Box 2001
Mechanicsburg, PA 17055
Rolls-Royce Enthusiasts Club
6 Montacuta Road
Tunbridge Wells,
Kent, TN2 5QP, England

Rolls-Royce Section of Vintage Sports Car Club
The Malt House
Bewdley, Worcs., England

Stevens-Duryea

Stevens-Duryea Associates
Warwick Eastward,
3565 Newhaven Road
Pasadena, CA 91107

Studebaker

Studebaker Automobile Society
50 Hickory Drive
East Hartford, CT 06118
Antique Studebaker Club
P.O. Box 142
Monrovia, CA 91016
Studebaker Automobile Club of America
P.O. Box 5036
Hemet, CA 92343
The Studebaker Driver's Club, Inc.
8330 Moberly Ln.
Dallas, TX 75227

Willys

Willys Club of America
137 Plymouth Ave.
Oreland, PA 19075
The Willys-Overland-Knight Registry
241 Orchard Dr.
Dayton, OH 45419

Classic Car Clubs of America

Full Classic Marked:*
Part Classic Marked: in Detail
Non Classic Marked: No

A.C.*
Adler—Please apply.
Alfa Romeo*
Alvis—Speed 20, 25 and 4.3 litre.
Amilcar—Supercharged
Sports
Model*
Others, please apply.
Apperson—No
Armstrong Siddeley—Please apply.
Aston-Martin—Ulster and Mark 2
Team cars*
Others, please apply.
Auburn—All Classic, except 6 cyl.
Austin (American)—No
Audi—No
Austro-Daimler*
Autovia—No

Bay State—No
Bentley*
Blackhawk*
B.M.W.* 327, 328 and 335 only.
Brewster—Heart Front Fords and one Heart Front Buick*
Bucciali*
Bugatti*
Buick—No, except one custom by Smith Bros.

Cadillac—All 1925 thru 1935*
All 12's and 16's*
1936-1942—All 70, 72, 75, 80, 85, 90*
All others are No, except five individual. 60's customs.

Case—No
Chandler—No
Chevrolet—No
Chrysler—1926 thru 1930 Imperial 80* 1931 Imp. 8 Series C.G.
1932-C.G. and C.L. 1933-C.L.
1934-C.W.-1935-C.W. & 5
Newports and 6 Thunderbolts*
All other—No
Citroen—No
Cleveland—No
Cole—No
Continental 1933 and 1934—No
Continental Lincoln* Thru 1948.
Cord*
Cunningham*

Dagmar—25-70 Model only*
Daimler—Please apply.
Darracq—8 cyl. cars and 4 litre, 6-cyl.*
Others—No
Davis—No
Delage—4 cyl. cars No
Others, please apply.
Delahaye—4 cyl. cars—No
Others, please apply.
Delaunay Belleville—6 cyl. cars*
Others—No
De Soto—No
Devaux—No
Diana—No
Doble*
Dodge—No
Dorris*

Dort—No

Duesenberg*

du Pont*

Durant—No

Elcar—No

Erskine—No

Essex—No

Excelsior—Please apply.

Falcon Knight—No

Farman—Please apply.

Fiat—Please apply.

Flint—No

Ford—No

Franklin—all models* except 1933-34

Olympic Sixes which are No

Frazer Nash—Please apply.

Gardner—No

Graham—No

Graham Paige—No, except 1929 Graham Paige, LeBaron, D.C. Phaeton and 1930 G.P. Erdman and Rossi Conv. Vict.

Gray—No

Hansa Lloyd—No

Haynes—No

Hispano Suiza*

Horch*

Hotchkiss—Please apply.

Hudson—No, except 2 Biddle & Smart bodied "Greater Super Sixes."*

Hupmobile—No

Invicta*

Isotta Fraschini*

Itala*

Jensen—Please apply.

Jewett—No

Jordan—Speedway Series 'Z'* only.

All others—No

Kissel—1925 and 1926, 1927—8-75, 1928, 8-90 and 8-90 White Eagle; 1929—8-126 and 8-90 White Eagle, 1930—8-126, 1931—8-126*

All others—No

La Fayette—No

Lagonda*, except Rapier, which is No

Lammas-Graham—No

Lanchester—Please apply.

Lancia—Please apply.

La Salle—1927 thru 1933* 1934 on—No

Lexington—No

Lincoln—All K., L., K.A. and K.B.*

1941—168H and 1942—268H* Zephyrs—No

Locomobile—All models 48 and 90, 1927—8-80, 1928—8-80, 1929—8-80 and 8-88*

All others—No

Marmon—All 16 cylinder* 1931—88 and Big 8, 1930—Big 8, 1928—E75, 1927—75, 1925 and 1926—74*

Others—No

Marquette—No

Maxwell—No

Mayback*

McFarlan*

Mercedes Benz—All 230 and up, and S., S.S., S.S.,., S.S.K.L., Grosser and Mannheim*

Mercer*

M.G.—K3 Magnette*
  Others, please apply.

Minerva—4 cyl. cars—No.
  Others*

Moon—if Custom, please apply.
  Others—No

Nash—No

Oakland—No

Oldsmobile—No

Opel—No

Overland—No

Packard—All sixes and eights

1925 thru 1931 are *
  All twelves are*, 1932—
    900 (Light eight) is No.
    All 1932—901, 902, 903,
    904, 905 and 906 cars
    are*, as are all 1933 and
    1934 cars, 1935 etc. follows:

Classic
1935
1200, 1201, 1202, 1203, 1204, 1205, 1207 and 1208

1936
1400, 1401, 1402, 1403, 1404, 1405, 1407 and 1408

1937
1500, 1501, 1502-1506, 1507 and 1508
1938
1603, 1604, 1605, Super 1607 and 1608
1939
1705 Super 1707 and 1708
1940
1806, 1807 and 1808 One-Eighty
1941
1906, 1907 and 1908 One-Eighty
1942

Super One-Eighty 2006, 2007 and 2008
Non-Classic
1935
120 8 cyl
1936
120-B 8 cyl
1937
115C 6 cyl., 120C 8 cyl., 120CD 8 cyl., 138CD 8 cyl.
1938
1600 6 cyl., 1601 8 cyl., 1601D 8 cyl. 1602 8 cyl.
1939
1700 6 cyl., One-Twenty, 1701 8 cyl., 1702 8 cyl. Super 1703 8 cyl.

1940
One-Ten, 1900 6 cyl., One-Twenty, 1901 8 cyl., One-Sixty, 1903 8 cyl., 1904 8 cyl., 1905 8 cyl., Clipper Eight, 8 cyl.
1942
Clipper Six, 2000 6 cyl., 2010 6 cyl., 2020 6 cyl., Clipper

Eight, 2001 8 cyl., 2011 8 cyl., 2021 8 cyl., Super One-Sixty, 2003 8 cyl., 2023 8 cyl., 2004 8 cyl., 2005 8 cyl., 2055 8 cyl., 2030 8 cyl.

Paige—No

Peerless—Series 60, 1926-1928 and Custom 8, 1930 and 1931 and DeLuxe Custom 8, 1932*
All others—No

Peugeot—Please apply.

Pierce-Arrow*

Plymouth—No

Pontiac—No

Railton—Please apply.

Renault—45 HP*
Others, please apply.

Reo—1933 Royale Custom 8, 1930 and 1931 Royale Custom 8 and Series 8-35 and 8-52 Elite 8*
All others—No

Revere*

Rickenbacker—No

Riley—please apply.

Roamer—1925—8-88, 6-54e and 4-75, 1926—4-75e and 8-88, 1927, 1928, 1929—8.88, 1929—8-125*

All others—No

Rockne—No

Rohr*

Rollin—No

Rolls-Royce*

Roosevelt—No

Ruxton*

Salmson—No

Squire*

S.S. Jaguar—SS1, SS90 and SS100*

Star—No

Stearns Knight*

Sterling Knight—No

Stevens Duryea*

Steyr—Please apply.

Studebaker—No

Stutz*

Sunbeam—8 cyl. and 3 twin cam*
Others—No

Sunbeam Talbot—No

Talbot—105 and 110 models*
Others—No

Tatra—Please apply.

Terraplane—No

Triumph—Dolomite 8 and

Gloria 6 models*
Others—No

Vauxhall—25-70 and 30-98*
Others—No

Velie—No

Viking—No

Voisin*

Westcott—No

Whippet—No

Wills Saint Claire—All 1925 and 1926*

Willys—No

Willys Knight—No

Windsor—No

Milestone Car Society Eligible Cars

AC Aceca...............1955-61
AC Buckland Open Tourer
...............................1949
AC (Shelby) Cobra ...1962-67
Alfa Romeo Giulietta
Spyder 1956-64
Alfa Romeo Giulietta/Giulia
Sprint Speciale 1959-61
Alfa Romeo 6C 2500 Super
Sport 1949
Allard Series J2, K2,
K3.......................1946-56
Apollo 1963-66
Arnolt Bristol..........1954-62
Aston Martin 1948-63
Aston Martin DB4, DB5, DB6
(All)......................1964-67
Austin Healey 100-6 .1956-59
Austin Healey 3000 ..1959-67
Austin Healey 100/ 100M
...........................1953-56
Bentley (All)...........1946-64
BMW 507 1957-59
Bugatti Type 101 1951
Buick Riviera..1949; 1963-65
Buick Skylark..........1953-54
Cadillac Eldorado.........1953
Cadillac Eldorado Brougham
................................1957-58
Cadillac Eldorado.1955; 1967
Cadillac Sixty Special 1948-49
Cadillac Sixty-One Coupe
(Fastback) 1948-49
Cadillac Sixty-Two Sedanet,
Conv., DeVille 1948-49
Chevrolet Bel Air V8 Hardtop
& Convertible 1955
Chevrolet Corvette 1953-58;
1960; 1962; 1964
Chevrolet Corvette, Coupe
Only 1963
Chevrolet Nomad.....1955-57

Chrysler 300 (Through "G"
Series) 1955-61
Chrysler Town & Country
...........................1946-50
Cisitalia GT (Pininfarina)
....1946-49
Citroen DS & ID 19 .1955-64
Continental Mark II ..1956-57
Corvair Monza Spyder 1962-64
Crosley Hotshot/SS..1950-52
Cunningham............1951-55
Daimler DE-36 (Custom
Built) 1949-53
Daimler 2.5 Special Sport
Conv.....................1949-53
Delage D.6 Sedan 1946-49
Delahaye Type 135, 175,
180......................1946-51
Dual Ghia...............1956-58
Facel Vega V-8........1954-64
Ferrari V-12 (All Front
Engined) 1947-67
Ford Skyliner (Retractable)
...........................1957-59
Ford Sportsman.......1946-48
Ford Thunderbird.....1955-57
Frazer Manhattan.....1947-50
Gaylord 1955-57
Healey Silverstone ...1949-50
Hudson (All) 1948-49
Hudson Hornet........1951-54
Imperial.................1955-56
Jaguar XK 120.........1948-53
Jaguar Mark V Drophead 1951
Jaguar Mark VII and '54 Mark
VII M.....................1951-54
Jaguar XK 140.........1954-57
Jaguar Mark VIII......1956-57
Jaquar Mark IX........1958-61
Jaguar Mark X.........1962-64
Jaguar XK 150.........1958-61
Jaguar 3.4/3.8 Sedans 1957-64

Studebaker Starlight Coupe (All Models) 1947-49
Studebaker Convertible (All Models)..................1947-49
Studebaker Starlight Coupe (Six & V-8) 1953-54
Studebaker Starliner Hardtop (Six & V-8) 1953-54
Talbot Largo 4.5 (All)1946-54
Triumph TR2/TR3 ...1953-63
Tucker 1948
Volvo P1800S 2-Door Coupe 1961-67
Willys-Overland Jeepster.................1948-51
Woodill Wildfire 1952-58

Appendix C
Restoration Services

Aluminum Bodies

Grand Prix SSR Co.
36 Rt. 25A
E. Setauket, NY 11733
516-751-8700
Specialize in complete aluminum bodies, metal fabricating, heliarc welding, etc.

Griswold Co.
1809 San Pablo Ave.
Berkeley, CA 94702
415-527-5818
Aluminum bodies, metal fabricating, heliarc welding etc.

Auctions

Christie Manson & Woods U.S.A. Ltd.
867 Madison Ave.
New York, NY 10021
212-744-4017

Collector Auto Auction Co. Inc.
5020 Main St.
Dayton, OH 45415
513-275-7450

Hudson & Marshall Inc.
1 Baconsfield Park
Macon, GA 31211
912-743-1511
800-841-9400
800-342-2666 (in GA)

Kruse Classic Auction Co. Inc.
300 South Union St.
Auburn, IN 46706
219-925-4004

Radcliffe Auction Co.
1100 E. MacArthur Rd.
Wichita, KS 67216

Sotheby Parke-Bernet Inc.
980 Madison Ave.
New York, NY 10021
212-879-8300

Badges-Emblems-Mascots

I. Markovits Ltd.
1,2,3, Cobbold Mews,
London W12, England
743 1131/1132/1313
*Restoring, re-enameling and
repainting vintage car badges.*

Pulfer & Williams
Robbins Rd., R.F.D. 1
Rindge, NH 03461
603-899-5659
*Emblems, nameplates, mas-
cots, motometers, cloisonne
emblems restored.*

Bearings-Poured Babbit

The Babbit Pot
RD #1, East River Road
Fort Edward, NY 12828
518-747-4277

Harkin Machine Shop
115 1st Ave. NW
Watertown, SD 57201
605-886-7880

P & K Bearing
Sales and Service
5446 Penn Ave.
Pittsburgh, PA 15206

Terrill Machine Co.
Rt. 2
DeLeon, TX 76444
817-893-2610

Books and Manuals

Tom Bonsall Literature
Box 7298
Arlington, VA 22207
202-234-1242

Classic Motorbooks
P.O. Box 1
Osceola, WI 54020
800-826-6600
*Complete Stock of Books and
Manuals*

Robert Bentley Inc.
872 Massachusetts Ave.
Cambridge, MA 02139

Bookman Dan
P.O. Box 13492
Baltimore, MD 21203

R. Gordon & Co. Inc.
Auto Books and Magazines
12 E. 55th St.
New York, NY 10022
212-759-7443

Hemmings Bookshelf
Box 76
Bennington, VT 05201

The Kruse Green Book
c/o Kruse Classic Auction Co.
300 South Union St.
Auburn, IN 46706

*Market Prices of Antique and
Classic Cars*

Rumbleseat Press
6639 Blucher Ave.
Van Nuys, CA 91406

All Ford Material

Crank-en Hope Publica-
tions
Blairsville, PA 15717
412-459-8853
*Reprinted Manuals and
Catalogs*

John W. Barnes, Jr. Pub-
lishing
Box 323
Scarsdale, NY 10583

Old Car Value Guide
910 Tony Lama
El Paso, TX 79915
915-592-5713

TAB Books Inc.
Box 40
Blue Ridge Summit, PA 17214

Nat Adelstein
102 Farnsworth Ave.
Bordentown, NJ 08505
609-888-1000
Original Literature

Brass Restoration

Chris Music
2406 W. Stuart
Fort Collins, CO 80526
303-493-2245

The Valley Forge Restoration
P.O. Box 1133
Apache Junction, AZ 85220

Car Covers

Warren Cox
P.O. Box 216
Lakewood, CA 90713
213-421-2884

What's Your Bag
714 E. Broadway
Glendale, CA 91205
213-240-7654

J. C. Whitney
1917 Archer Ave.
P.O. Box 8410
Chicago, IL 60680

Electrical Systems

Harnesses Unlimited
P.O. Box 435
Wayne, PA 19087
no telephone

J.M.S. Antique Auto Parts Co.
3915 Kirkwood Highway
Wilmington, DE 19808
302-995-1131
Custom harnesses & wiring supplies; custom braiding service.

Pacific Conduit & Cable Corp.
1725 Standard Ave.
Glendale, CA 91201
213-245-1013
Auto loom, auto harness braiding, colored cotton braided wire.

Wayne Schlotthauer
Wiring Diagrams
5815 Nielsen Drive
Paradise, CA 95969

The Wire King Inc.
P.O. Box 222
N. Olmsted, OH 44070
216-398-6200

Engine Rebuilding

Classic Auto Restoration
22456 Orchard Lake Road
Farmington, MI 48204
313-477-4767
800-521-6084

Drake's Engine Shop
259 Lee Road
Rochester, NY 14606
716-458-0217

Doug's Engine & Machine Shop
671 Reed St.
Santa Clara, CA 95050
408-727-1818

Grand Prix SSR Co.
36 Rte. 25A
E. Setauket, NY 11733
516-751-8700
*Specialize in high performance
and racing engines.*

Harkin Machine Shop
115 1st Ave. NW
Watertown, SD 57201
605-886-7880

Page's Model A Garage
Haverhill, NH 03765
603-989-5592
*Model A Ford and early V8
Ford engine rebuilding*

**Pioneer Valley Model A
Ford**
Warren Paul
178 Telegraph Ave.
Chicopee, MA 01020
413-533-2927
Model A engine rebuilding.

**The Restoration Engine
Shop**
R.D. 1, Box 228
Jamesburg, NJ 08821
201-521-1128

Engine Turning (Damascening)

Herb Newport
Box 100
Wittman, MD 21676

Financing

Maryland National Bank
Custom Lending Dept.
8400 Baltimore Blvd.
College Park, MD 20740
301-441-3201

Gaskets

Gerald J. Lettieri
132 Old Main St.
Rocky Hill, CT 06067
203-529-7177

Ace Gasket Co.
244 W. Lincoln Ave.
Mt. Vernon, NY 10550
914-664-3710
Gaskets Made To Order

Head Gasket Company
164 South Park
San Francisco, CA 94107
415-397-3111

L.A.D.C.
Box 14031
7900 Quivira Road
Lenexa, KS 66215
913-492-9465

Gauge Repairs

Bob's Speedometer
15255 Grand River Ave.
Detroit, MI 48227
313-272-1050

**The Temperature Gauge
Guy**
45 Prospect St.
Essex Jct., VT 05452

J. Lynch
33 Loomis St.
Little Falls, NY 13365
no telephone
*Gauges, sending units, switches,
hydro-electric window cylinders
repaired.*

Nisonger Corp.
35 Bartels Place
New Rochelle, NY 10801
914-235-2400

Paul C. Sullivan
4311 Sunset Blvd.
Los Angeles, CA 90029

Instruments Restored

John E. Marks
The Old Bakery, Windmill St.,
Tunbridge Wells,
Kent TN2 4UU, England
(0892) Tunbridge Wells 25899
Vintage Restorations of Instruments and Clocks

Gus Scheuer
31 Dunwoodie Place
Greenwich, CT 06830
Instrument dial face restoration.

Insurance

American Collectors Insurance
P.O. Box 15465
Philadelphia, PA 19149
609-234-2552

Classic Insurance Agency
4399 Atlanta Road
Smyra, GA 30080
404-435-4477

J.C. Taylor
8701 West Chester Pike
Upper Darby, PA 19082
215-853-1300

James A. Grundy Insurance
500 Office Center Drive
Fort Washington, PA 19034
215-628-3100

Condon and Skelly Insurance Brokers
P.O. Drawer "A"
Willingboro, NJ 08046
609-871-1212

Leather

Connolly Bros. Ltd.
39-43 Chalton St.
London NW1, England

Classic Leather & Vinyl Care

P.O. Box 218
Centerport, NY 11721
516-757-4405

Harold Coker
1600 E. 25th St.
Chattanooga, TN 37411
800-251-6336

Hides Inc.
P.O. Box 30
Hackettstown, NJ 07840
Fine Upholstery Leather

Bill Hirsch
396 Littleton Ave.
Newark, NJ 07103
201-243-2858
"Bridge of Weir" leather.

Chuck Pelton
2466 Sunset Terrace
Union Lake, MI 48085

Leather Preservative

Lexol Corp.
West Caldwell, NJ 07006

Tachmaster
Lyndonville, VT 05851

Leather Straps & Hardware

IMCADO Manufacturing Co.
P.O. Box 452
148 Pine St.
Dover, DE 19901
302-734-4177

Machining

Bloomfield Foundry Inc.
25 Broadway
Clark, NJ 07066
201-862-2278

Walter Will
301 E. 195th St.
Euclid, OH 44119
216-531-1631

Magazines

Antique Motor News
919 South St.
Long Beach, CA 90805

Automobile Quarterly Publications
245 W. Main St.
Kutztown, PA 19530

Cars and Parts
P.O. Box 482
Sidney, OH 45367

Hemmings Motor News
Box 100
Bennington, VT 05201

Special Interest Autos
Box 196
Bennington, VT 05201

Old Cars
Iola, WI 54945

Magneto/Ignition Coil Repairs

George Pounden
1520 High School Road
Sebastopol, CA 94572
707-823-3824

Metal Fabrication

Chester Auto Restoration Service
Perry St.
Chester, NJ 07930
201-879-5041

Mirrors-Resilvered

Dan Tilstone
29 N. Delaware Rim Drive
Yardley, PA 19067

Parts

Antique Auto Parts Inc.
9113 E. Garvey Ave.
Rosemead, CA 91770
213-288-2121

Burchill Antique Auto Parts
4150 24 Ave. (U.S. 25 N.)
Port Huron, MI 48060
313-385-3838

Classic Cars Inc.
Maple Terrace
Hibernia, NJ 07842
201-627-1975

Egge Machine Company
8403 Allport Ave.
Santa Fe Springs, CA 90670
213-945-3419

Rick's Antique Auto
Box 662
Shawnee Mission, KS 66201
913-722-5252

J.C. Whitney & Co.
1917 Archer Ave.
P.O. Box 8410
Chicago, IL 60680

Alfa Romeo Parts

Grand Prix SSR Co.
36 Route 25A
E. Setauket, N.Y. 11733
516-751-8700

Auburn Parts

Auburn/Cord Parts
604 South "G" St.
Wellington, KS 67152
316-326-7751

Frank Heiss Antique Autos
1230 U.S. 130
Westville, NJ 08093
609-848-6005

Brass Parts

Monty Holmes
3653 Commodore Way
Seattle, WA 98199

Bugatti Parts

Parthenon Motors Ltd.
204 Dinn Road
San Antonio, TX 78218

Chevrolet Parts

Jim Tygart
Obsolete Chevrolet Parts Co.
Inc.
202 North Taylor St.
Nashville, GA 31639
912-686-5812
Specialized Auto Parts
7130 Capitol St.
Houston, TX 77011
713-928-3707

Cord Parts (See Auburn)

Corvette Parts

**T. Michaelis Corvette
Supplies Inc.**
Rt. 1, 424 East
Napoleon, OH 43545
800-537-3050
David N. Rosen
364 Tompkins St.
Cortland, NY 13045
The Vette Shop
12115 Self Plaza
Dallas, TX 75218
214-328-3124

English Car Parts

**The Complete Au-
tomobilist Ltd.**
39 Main St., Baston,
Peterborough, England
07786-312

Ferrari Parts

**David Clarke Ferrari Or-
ganization**
Graypaul Motors Limited
Charnwood Rd.
Shepshed, Leics., England
FAF Motorcars Inc.
3862 Stephens Court
Tucker, GA 30084
404-939-5464
Grand Prix SSR Co.
36 Route 25A
E. Setauket, NY 11733
516-751-8700

Ford Parts

A & L Parts Specialities
P.O. Box 301
Canton, CT 06019
**Antique Auto & Parts by
Pete**
2144 W. Superior St.
Chicago, IL 60612
312-486-1910
Antique Auto Parts
173 Hotchkiss St.
Jamestown, NY 14701
Model T Ford Parts
Antique Car Parts
Harold E. Severson
9400 S.E. 41st St.
Portland, OR 97222
503-659-2821
Beam Distributors
231 South St.
P.O. Box 524
Davidson, NC 28036
704-892-5205
Bob's Antique Auto Parts
P.O. Box 1856
7826 Forest Hills Road
Rockford, IL 61110
815-633-7244

Dennis Carpenter
P.O. Box 26398
Charlotte, NC 28213
704-786-8139
V-8 Reproductions

Newood for Fords
Box 79
Luna, NM 87824
602-339-4350

Pat Day Company
310 Rigsbee Ave.
Box 489
Durham, NC 27702
919-688-2620

Bob Drake
7838-40 Alabama Ave.
Canoga Park, CA 91304
213-346-6199

Fleet Supply Corp.
2896 Central
Detroit, MI 48209
313-843-2200

Ford Parts Obsolete Inc.
1320 W. Willow
Long Beach, CA 90810

Gaslight Auto Parts Inc.
Box 291, Rt. 68 S.
Urbana, OH 43078
513-652-2145

Glazier's Mustang Barn Inc.
531 Wambold Road
Souderton, PA 18964
215-723-9674

Greenland Enterprises
P.O. Box 332
Verdugo City, CA 91046
213-249-8344

Mal's "A" Sales
4968 S. Pacheco Blvd.
Martinez, CA 94553
415-228-8180

Mark Auto Co. Inc.
Layton, NJ 07851
201-948-4157

Dean McDonald
R.R. 3, Box 61
Rockport, IN 47635
812-359-4965

Midwest Auto Parts Co.
P.O. Box 1081
Galesburg, IL 61401

Restorations & Reproductions
1133 S.E. 199th St.
Portland, OR 97233
503-667-4529

Page's Model A Garage
Haverhill, NY 03765
603-989-5592

Rick's Antique Auto
Box 662
Shawnee Mission, KS 66201
913-722-5252

Snyder's Antique Auto Parts, Inc.
12925 Woodworth Road
New Springfield, OH 44443
216-549-5313

Specialized Auto Parts
7130 Capitol St.
Houston, TX 77011
713-928-3707

Syverson Cabinet Co.
2301 Rand Road
Palatine, IL 60067
"Wood Parts that Fit to A T"

V-8 Shop Inc.
21917 Aurora Road
Bedford Hts., OH 44146
216-526-7718

Jaguar Parts

Bassett's Restorations and Supplies
P.O. Box 145
Peace Dale, RI 02883
401-789-9378

Engel Imports Inc.
618 E. Crosstown Parkway
Kalamazoo, MI 49001
800-253-4080

Bill Tracy
3179 Woodland Ave.
Alexandria, VA 22309
703-360-6652

Welsh's Jaguar Enterprises
1108 Oak Grove Ave.
Steubensville, OH 43952
614-282-8649

G.M. Car Parts

G.M. Obsolete Parts
98 Homestead St.
Albany, NY 12203
518-438-1555

Rick's Antique Auto
Box 662
Shawnee Mission, KS 66201
913-722-5252

M.G. & English Car Parts

Abingdon Spares, Ltd.
1329 Highland Ave.
Needham, MA 02192
617-444-9235

British Restoration Parts
1808 Oak
Kansas City, MO 64108
816-471-2776

Long's British Parts Ltd.
Box 19832
Kansas City, MO 64141

L.A.D.C.
Box 14031
7900 Quivira Road
Lenexa, KS 66215
913-492-9465

Moss Motors, Ltd.
7200 Hollister Ave.
Goleta, CA 93017
805-968-1041

Sports and Classics
750 Canal St.
Stamford, CT 06903
203-327-2775

Packard Parts

Classic Cars Inc.
Maple Terrace
Hibernia, NJ 07842
201-627-1975

Pistons

Jahn's Quality Pistons Inc.
2662 Lacy St.
Los Angeles, CA 90031
213-225-8177

Judson Mfg. Co. Inc.
1345 Byberry Road
Cornwells Hts., PA 19020

Egge Machine Company
8403 Allport Ave.
Santa Fe Springs, CA 90670
213-945-3419

Plating & Polishing

Ace Chrome Plating Co.
728 W. Highland Ave.
Milwaukee, WI 53233
414-273-6596
*Chrome plating, most metals
including die cast*

Bill's Metal Polishing
Davis Rd. & Camden Ave.
Magnolia, NJ 08049
609-784-1019

Davison Plating Co.
P.O. Box 21
Davison, MI 48423
313-653-4474
Copper, nickel, chrome and brass plating on antique and classic cars

Graves Plating Co.
Industrial Park
P.O. Box 1052H
Florence, AL 35630
205-764-9487

Daisson D. Hickel
23 George St.
Newark, NJ 07105
201-589-8686

High-Grade Plating Co.
1245 W. 2nd St.
Pomona, CA 91766
714-629-6616

Chrome or nickel plating for antique cars; windshield frame and grille shell repair; headlight and reflector restoration

Hygrade Polishing & Plating Co.
2207 41st Ave.
Long Island City, NY 11101
212-392-4082

J and J Chrome Plating and Metal Finishing Corp.
101 Orange Ave.
West Haven, CT 06516
203-934-8510
Triple-plate show chrome

The Khrome Shoppe
509 Grace St.
Poteau, OK 74953
918-647-9973

Modern Polishing & Plating
242 S. 12th ST.
Newark, NJ 07107
201-638-8178
Show chrome for antique cars.

O'Donnell Plating Co. Inc.
41 Mill St.
Springfield, MA 01108
413-736-4303
Custom chrome plating, complete metal finishing service.

Qual Krom
28 Orchard Pl.
Poughkeepsie, NY 12601
914-473-4410

Watervliet Plating Co.
911 11th St.
Watervliet, NY 12189
518-273-1095

Radio Repairs

Carl Heuther
54 Hobbs Road
Pelham, NH 03076
603-635-3048
Pre-1957 car radios

Dan Packard
8 Florence Road
Marblehead, MA 01945
617-631-2449

Radio West
1429 Santa Monica Blvd.
Santa Monica, CA 90404
213-393-3974
1930-1960 radios, domestic & foreign.

Glen Thome
917 Delaware Ave.
Elyria, OH 44035
no telephone
Radios repaired; any model year

Rubber

The Complete Auto-mobilist Ltd.
39 Main ST.,
Baston,
Nr. Peterborough, PE69NX,
England
07786-312

Metro Moulded Parts
3031 2nd St. N.
Minneapolis, MN 55411
612-521-0123

Wefco Rubber Mfg. Corp.
1655 Euclid Ave.
Santa Monica, CA 90404
213-393-0303

Rust Removal

Redi-Strip
Locations throughout U.S.
213-944-9915 for nearest location

W.T. Tyrrel-PF47 Rust Remover
Box 98-RG
East Northport, NY 11731
516-261-5380

Tip Sandblast Equipment Mfg.
17 Kenmore Ave
P.O. Box 2739
Youngstown, OH 44507
216-743-9733

Lehman General Sales Co.
1835 Stelzer Road
Columbus, OH 43219
614-471-0533

Skybrite Co.—"OSPHO"
3125 Perkins Ave.
Cleveland, OH 44114

Shock Absorber Restoration

Five Points Classic Auto Shocks
7471 Slater, Unit G
Huntington, Beach, CA 92647
714-842-0707

J.D. Duke
1611 Brentwood
Athens, TN 37303
no telephone
Model A shocks rebuilt

Steering Wheels & Repairs

Jim Ellis
4143 Gunderson Road N.E.
Pulsbo, WA 98370
206-697-1471

Bill Peters Restorations
37 DeKoven Court
Brooklyn, NY 11230
212-434-7721 NO
Plastic, hard rubber & wood steering wheels.

Mark Wallach Ltd.
27 New St.
Nyack, NY 10960
914-358-8179

Timing Chains

Ramsey Products Corp.
724 Gesco St.
Charlotte, NC 28208
704-376-6477

John Pinizzatto
68 Angola Road, Box 266
Cornwall, NY 12518
914-534-2014

Tires

Bill's Antique Tires
P.O. Box 176
7526 Kay Lynn St.
Stanley, KS 66223
913-897-2685

Coker Tire Co.
1600 E. 25th St.
Chattanooga, TN 37411
800-251-6336

John Kelsey
Kelsey Tire Co. Inc.
Box 564
Camdenton, MO 65020
314-346-2506

Lester Tire Co.
637 N.W. 12th Ave.
Deerfield Beach, FL 33441
305-421-0940

Lucas Automotive—West
2850 Temple Ave.
Long Beach, CA 90806
213-595-6721

Lucas Automotive—East
2141 W. Main
Springfield, OH 45504
513-324-1773

Universal Tire Co.
2650 Columbia Ave.
Lancaster, PA 17603
717-397-5184

Willie's Antique Tires
5257 W. Diversey Ave.
Chicago, IL 60639
312-622-4037

Titles & Registrations

Mac Charlson
113 Hinsdale
Mattydale, NY 13211

Jim Parkinson
P.O. Box 4082
Sunnyside, NY 11104
212-937-0985

Trailers

John E. Brown Motors Ltd.
Gorrie, Ontario, Canada
519-335-3325

C & C Mfg. Co.
300 S. Church St.
Hazleton, PA 18201
717-454-0819
800-233-6191

G. Sturgeon
3209 Erie Dr.
Orchard Lake, MI 48033
313-682-1197

Thomas O. Hudson
Tommy's Trailers
P.O. Box 71
Ada, OK 74820
405-332-7785

Don Jensen Enterprises
Humboldt, IA 50548
515-332-3343

Trailex, Inc.
60 Industrial Park Drive
Canfield, OH 44406
216-533-6814

Wells Cargo, Inc.
1503 W. McNaughton St.
P.O. Box 728-197
Elkhart, IN 46515
800-348-7553

Transporting

Horseless Carriage Carriers Inc.
61 Iowa Ave.
Paterson, NJ 07503
201-742-2692
800-631-7796

Passport Transport Ltd.
9479 Aerospace Dr.
St. Louis, MO 63134
314-426-6777

Upholstery & Top Material

Antique Fabric and Trim Co.
Rt. 2 - Box 870
Cambridge, MN 55008
612-742-4025

Bill Hirsch
396 Littleton Ave.
Newark, NJ 07103
201-243-2858

Fred Kanter
Packard Industries
76R Monroe St.
Boonton, NJ 07005
201-334-2400

LeBaron Bonney Co.
14 Washington St.
Amesbury, MA 01913
617-388-3811

Pearson & Marzian Inc.
501 E. St. Catherine St.
Louisville, KY 40203
502-585-2475

Charles Wes. Sayler
P.O. Box 438
Kearney, MO 64060
816-676-2571

Stitts
Rt. #3
Churchtown, PA 17555
215-445-6821

Western Hide-Tex
Box 2133 Encinal Station
Sunnyvale, CA 94087
408-733-7790

Upholstery & Top Patterns

Carters Cut and Cover Shop
Box 80
Beardstown, IL 62618
217-323-1832

Morris Upholstery
1870 Spring Rd.
Carlisle, PA 17013
717-249-3244

Wood Wheels

Amarya Crafts
147 Carolynn Road
Mabank, TX 75147

Bob Calimer
30 E. North St.
Waynesboro, PA 17268
717-762-5056

Wire Wheels

Dayton Wheel Products Inc.
1147 S. Broadway St.
Dayton, O 45408
513-461-1707
Wire wheel rebuilding.

Wheel Repair Service Inc. of New England
317 Southbridge St.
Auburn, MA 01501
617-799-6551
Wire wheel rebuilding.

Woodgraining

John R. Guerin
221 Herbert Ave.
Fanwood, NJ 07023
201-889-6863

Neal Rogers
6214 Lynbrook
Houston, TX 77057

Wood Top Bows

Oak Bows
122 Ramsey Ave.
Chambersburg, PA 17201
717-264-2602

C.B. Darcy
73 Scudders Lane
Glenhead, NY 11545
no telephone
Custom automobile woodwork

Wayne M. Baker
12 Tracy's Pathe
Marshfield, MA 02050
617-837-9357

Index

Index